Stanis's Guide to a Purrfect Life

Everyday Wisdom from a Cozy Cat

Stanis the Cat & Elisa Colarossi

Andrews McMeel
PUBLISHING®

Stanis's Guide to a Purrfect Life

The authorised representative in the EEA is Simon and Schuster Netherlands BV, Herculesplein 96 3584 AA Utrecht, Netherlands. (info@simonandschuster.nl)

Andrews McMeel Publishing
a division of Andrews McMeel Universal
1130 Walnut Street, Kansas City, Missouri 64106

www.andrewsmcmeel.com

26 27 28 29 30 RLP 10 9 8 7 6 5 4 3 2 1

ISBN: 979-8-8816-1194-1

Library of Congress Control Number: 2026940235

Editor: Katie Gould
Art Director: Holly Swayne
Production Editor: Elizabeth A. Garcia
Production Manager: Tamara Haus

FSC www.fsc.org MIX Paper | Supporting responsible forestry FSC® C102842

CONTENTS

INTRODUCTION . . . 1

MEET STANIS'S FRIENDS . . . 3

DAILY LIFE DELIGHTS . . . 19

PURRSONAL PHILOSOPHIES . . . 61

SELF-CARE WITH STANIS . . . 77

TRAVEL TALES . . . 97

MARVELOUS MEOWTHFULS . . . 115

ANTIQUE BOOKSHOP
Cat Legends
HISTORY
flowers
Herbs
CATOGRAPHY
WHISKERIA
Meow
@stanisthecat

INTRODUCTION

Hi! This is Stanis! If you don't know me yet, it's time that I introduce myself. I am a twelve-year-old black cat from Rome. I wrote this book with my very own paws, and I hope it will help cheer you up. I have many friends and tons of hobbies and passions! I'm cute, very round, and I always have a little tip for my friends (including you!).

And since we're friends, let me tell you a little more about myself . . .

The kitchen is where I shine! I love tomato sauce; it is my best recipe, and I love to pair it with fusilli or spaghetti, my two favorite shapes of pasta. I love fusilli because, in Italian, *fusa* means "purr," so as a cat, you can see why I love it! And why spaghetti? Well, when I was a kitten, I used to bite uncooked spaghetti noodles just for fun, so after trying them cooked, they have become a favorite of mine (and of course, they're even better than uncooked)!

I'm a very good gardener! I take care of my terrace regularly (and with lots of love). It's filled with wonderful herbs and lots of cute, small vegetables.

Red is my color! It suits me so well! I have my favorite apron in red, and most of my furniture is red as well. I just love it!

I read a lot of books! There is nothing better than curling up in my little chair and diving deep into intriguing mysteries and fascinating travel guides.

Jazz is absolutely my soundtrack to life! Wherever I go, jazz follows. In fact, a very cozy way to read this book is with my very own playlist, which you can find on page 29.

I love nature so much! Hanging out with flowers, trees, and my animal friends is my favorite way to spend time. Nature helps me understand how great our world is, and how important it is to take care of it.

Painting and crafting are very soothing passions of mine! With my little paws, I can make charming masterpieces (I don't think I'm that great, but sometimes my girlfriend, Corinna, calls me Meowchelangelo, and that makes me feel so good).

The simple things are the best! I try to live day by day, appreciating the small things we sometimes forget to notice or do in our busy lives: watching a pretty sunset unfold, buying flowers, or preparing a cozy meal. It's my very own secret to smiling every day, even when I'm blue.

purrs, naps, treats, repeat
Be happy!
FLOWERS
Reminder:
do the things that make you purr
Stanis the cat
Stanis' PLAYLIST
@stanisthecat

MEET Stanis's FRIENDS

You probably know them from my posts online, but just in case, I'd better introduce you to the best friends I could ever wish for. Even better, why don't they introduce themselves?!

@stanisthecat

CORINNA

Hi, dears! I'm Corinna, Stanis's girlfriend, and it's so nice to meet you! I have so many things in common with Stanis: for example, our love for jazz music and thrifting (I own a vintage shop called Vintage Paws you should really visit one day). I adore summer, going to the beach or the lake and enjoying the sun and the breeze. Stanis knows that my favorite flowers are pansies, and he's always so cute to gift them to me whenever he can. I'm very handy, so when something breaks or has a problem, I love to challenge myself to try to fix it. Whenever I don't succeed, Stanis is always ready to lend me a paw! If you meet me at a special event, you'll spot me thanks to my iconic glittery pink bag, my favorite accessory in the world!

Favorite food:
Margherita pizza

Favorite hobbies:
thrift shopping and making jewelry

How I deal with a bad day:
I have a proper spa day, like Stanis does (he said to me that he wrote about it in this book, and trust me, it does wonders!).

MAGRIPPA·LF·COSTERTIVM·FECIT
@stanisthecat

How I Met Corinna

This is the sweetest story you'll be hearing today! If you didn't know, I'm a cat who loves jazz music. It's my soundtrack when I cook or read, and this genre just makes me feel happy and at ease.

One evening, I was getting ready to go to my favorite jazz club, The Cool Beans, where not only are the cat jazz bands spectacular but also the atmosphere is so chic, and I like to think of myself as a chic cat with a tiny martini in my paws listening to smooth sax solos, you know?

I was listening to the band, enjoying my Pawsecco, when I suddenly heard the most wonderful voice: Corinna's! She was the best singer I'd ever heard! Yes, Corinna is a talented jazz singer, so it's no wonder that I fell in love with her immediately.

We went on a romantic date the following night, during which we had pizza and talked about everything we liked: jazz music, vintage shops, traveling, and eating good food. When I said to her that I was a good cook, she was so happy and very willing to try my tomato sauce! Corinna told me that she is the owner of the supercute Vintage Paws shop, where she sold second-paw clothes, cute vintage accessories, and everything special and forgotten. So cool, right?

After our date, I went to visit her at her shop, and wow! I lost myself in all the stunning and quirky things and brought a pot of my tomato sauce as a special gift to her. She absolutely loved it! Corinna, understandably so, loves my food so much and, as you know, preparing delicious dishes for your loved one is an incredible act of love—especially my spaghetti!

We decided to be a cute couple, and, oh, how many adventures we have had since then! We visited Paris, ran through Rome with my little red Vespa, ate pizza, and enjoyed slow breakfasts in the piazza. Corinna is the soulmate I wish for every cat in the world. We all deserve to have someone loving us and nurturing us. For those who haven't already found the Corinna in their life, don't worry. I'm certain that it will happen very, very soon. Stanis's word!

Stanis
@stanisthecat

REMO

Hello, friends! I'm Remo, Stanis's best friend! It's such an honor to meet you. Stanis told me I have a huge number of fans around the world (and maybe you reading are a new one), and so I feel like a VIP when I fly around, so thank you! I love spring and hanging out with Stanis; we do so many things together: cooking and going around for groceries and book shopping and even gardening. He's truly my best friend, and I'm so grateful for him! I love sunflowers—they just look so majestic—and when I want to feel super good, I dance to the rhythm of funk music (I've got some serious moves; you should see me!).

Favorite food:
bread with dips and spreads

Favorite hobby:
mapmaking

How I deal with a bad day:
I eat some sunflower seeds while watching a comfort TV show, and I take a slow walk in a place I like.

@stanisthecat

Windows' Tales from Stanis (and How I Met Remo)

There is a place in the house that truly comforts me and makes me feel like I have the whole world in my paws: the window. Big or small, it does not matter, as long as I can see what goes on outside! Flickering lights at night over wonderful views, all the birds flying around, the clouds making funny and lovely shapes, the sunsets and the sunrises; oh, there is so much to see!

That's how I met Remo! I was enjoying my fresh lemonade and the breeze of the evening at my window. At a certain point, this friendly, funny little pigeon joined me. He had some fresh bread, which he had just bought from the bakery (he isn't a fan of just crumbs; this guy is very adamant about bakery-bought bread, I know!) and wanted to take a little break—carrying a baguette does that when you're a tiny pigeon. So he said, "Ciao! Would you like to share a piece of bread while I take a little break?" I couldn't say no! But I had the best idea, so I grabbed a spread and offered him a glass of lemonade too. We had the best aperitif, looking at the pink, glowing sunset enveloping Rome. From that point on, we were super best friends!

Windows are magical: They give you a glimpse of beautiful things, and window gazing is one of the best pastimes out there. When you're a little bored around the house, stomping your paws from one room to another because you don't know what to do, head to the coziest window in your house and just spend a couple of minutes there. Doesn't matter the view you have, majestic or not (all views are majestic, in my opinion), but just let it lull you into a moment of beautiful peace and quiet, during which you can gaze at anything your attention is drawn to. It's so calming!

THREE FUN GAMES YOU CAN DO AT THE WINDOW:

- Spot the funniest-looking clouds and make up shapes and stories about them.
- Say hi to all the birds you see, like I did with Remo—you might even become friends with some.
- Take photos of different times of day or seasons, then make a nice collage to see how the views change over time.

STANIS
UNDER COVER CAT
MEOWSTER Chef
THE REAL HOUSE CAT
CATURDAY NIGHT LIVE
SILENT PAWS
PAW & ORDER
CATFLIX
PIZZA
@stanisthecat

VINO
@stanisthecat

CESARE

Hi, buddies! I'm Cesare, Stanis's friend! I'm a tabby cat. I have so much energy all the time, but don't worry, I nap a lot too. I love summer, so I can swim and enjoy all the outdoor activities! With Stanis, I enjoy playing card and board games for hours! I love Monopoly, Risk, Catan, and classic Italian card games; Stanis and I have tournaments throughout the year and we have so much fun. Of course, we include Remo, Corinna, and Ottavia as well! I like daffodils, and I always stop to take a photo when I see one. I listen to rock music; it gives me a lot of energy and makes me super ready for the day!

Favorite food:
roasted potatoes
(Stanis makes them so well.)

Favorite hobby:
practicing sports like swimming, running, and napping (that is considered a sport too!)

How I deal with a bad day:
I spend most of the day outside, if I can, or I wrap myself up in my blanket and play video games.

1
2
Photos
SCIEN
TRIPS
I ♥ TRAVEL
@stanisthecat

OTTAVIA

Hello, treasures! I'm Ottavia, the new addition to the group, but it's like I've know Stanis and his friends since forever! I'm a seagull, and I've lived around the world, but Rome is my home. I speak many languages, I love to travel, and you'll never see me without one of my very fashionable (thank you, Corinna) scarves. I'm so happy to have met my new friends—they truly are the best! We have so many fun adventures together, and I can't wait to have so many more. I love to fly over lavender fields, paint, and learn new languages. My luggage is always ready for the next adventure!

Favorite food:
french fries!

Favorite hobby:
watching clouds and their quirky shapes

How I deal with a bad day:
I write my thoughts in my little notebook and buy myself pretty flowers!

DAILY LIFE DELIGHTS

FRESCO ♥ FRESH
WE ♥ FRUIT & VEGGIES
FRUIT!
POMODORI
COCOMERO
@stanisthecat

MARKET ADVENTURES:
WHAT I BUY MONTHLY

Come with me for some produce shopping! I love me some market time. With all the colors, the sights, and the sounds it offers, especially here, where I live (Italian cats are louder than your average cat, you know), it's always a one-of-a-kind experience whenever I go! I've learned to buy my produce based on the seasons, which is great for the planet and for my recipes, which taste amazing, thanks to the freshness of the produce. And so, with my paws, I gently squeeze tomatoes to see if they are purrfect for my sauce, and if they are firmer, they'll be in my salad. Let's go shop, month by month, for the most purrfect veggies and fruits!

In **January** and **February** you'll want to buy broccoli, spinach, and cabbage, for making amazing stews, soups, and sides. Oranges and grapefruit are at their peak, and they are so good for vitamin-packed morning juices.

When spring hits in **March** and **April**, get ready for artichokes and asparagus! You can make delicious, springy dishes, savory tarts, and yummy pasta dishes. Strawberries start to appear and it makes me so happy.

The sun shines, the air is warmer, and the veggies get delicious. In **May** and **June**, buy green beans, zucchini, and tomatoes! It's my favorite time of the year, honestly: All the tomatoes are out, from the cherry to the San Marzano! Love it! Cherries and peaches start to timidly peek from around the corner and are usually very delicious already!

Summer is in full swing, and cucumbers, peppers, and eggplant are the main characters! I make roasted peppers during summer; their smoky flavor is just incredible! During **July** and **August**, it gets sweeter, too, because watermelon is in season! Whether cut into cubes, into salads, or by the slice, watermelon is an icon of summertime!

September and **October** are for leafy greens and for the last delicious veggies of the summer, but fruit starts to be the real superstar. Pears, grapes, and apples are in season, and I can't resist a sugary grape when I see it!

Cold but delicious, **November** and **December** focus on cruciferous veggies like brussels sprouts, and the fruit gets zesty; oranges, grapefruits, and lemons make a lovely comeback! Use the lemon for your final touch on pasta dishes or to make awesome limoncello at home.

WHAT I GROW IN MY GARDEN

My cute little terrace is always full of wonderful plants and flowers. Winter or spring, I love to take care of it the whole year-round. Walking in the morning with a coffee in paws and seeing all my green beauties truly fills my heart! I go to the garden center once or twice every season to buy what I need, and the rest is maintenance or shopping for more whenever I feel like I need more plants! Yes, I know, I'm that kind of cat—I always need more plants. Don't we all?!

Here is my planting schedule for my terrace!

SPRING is for
tulips, daisies, azaleas, and basil.

SUMMER is for sunflowers,
hydrangeas, jasmine, and oregano.

AUTUMN is for
pansies, roses, geraniums, and rosemary.

WINTER is for
cyclamen, sage, and snowdrops.

During summer, **I grow tomatoes too**! I buy the sprouts and put them in deep, large pots so they can grow big and healthy. The best tomato that is easy to grow (especially for its weight) is the cherry tomato. Purrfect for salads, or even a quick snack just like candy. Don't forget to attach the plants to a little trellis for stability.

Taking care of plants is a little difficult sometimes, as each one has specific needs and keeping up with many could become a proper job. That's why, when I'm at the garden center, I always ask for tips from the very wise cat working there. For example, for the best basil, you should never tear the leaves but instead use scissors, and only keep it in the sun for half a day. Succulents, on the other hand, love to sunbathe all day!

Stanis's List of the Tools You Need to Be the Best Gardener

- Trowel, for digging (but you can also use your paws)
- Watering can
- Spray bottle, for misting
- Gloves, the more colorful the better!
- Trellis and ties, for support
- Kneeling pad, for comfort

GARDEN
TERRA
@stanisthecat

@stanisthecat

Stanis Enjoys Spring

The last drops of rain are drying, the sun is timidly peeking out of the clouds, and the birds are singing loudly again—welcome to spring! I love springtime because I can have fun outside without sweating too much or feeling too cold. It is the purrfect season for lighthearted fun with your friends or on your own.

Spring is the charming season of renewal, and I always promise myself to enjoy it fully, starting with the many picnics I have with Corinna! She grabs a vintage blanket from her shop, I prepare some savory croissants with a slice of cheese and some strawberries, and we pick the best trees to set up our comfy spot. Butterflies come to say hi, and in the air, you can smell the flowers blossoming. It can't get more romantic than that.

Remo and I love to paint *en plein air* with watercolors, and we let nature become our muse, painting the fascinating landscape or focusing on a specific flower or tree. When it's sunny, we rent a rowboat and enjoy the gentle lull of the water, drifting across the lake and encountering ducks. At the end of the day, I play cards with Cesare on the terrace, savoring a little glass of red wine while we enjoy each other's company and the glowing sunset—our favorite!

Cooking is another fundamental part of why I love spring. Does that surprise anyone? This time of year, I focus on savory tarts; the best one I make is made with peas and zucchini (with some crumbled feta) and a little zest of lemon. It's so yummy and springy! Pasta, however, is where I shine, so with my paws, I whip up linguine with a creamy sauce of lemon and asparagus. It's super easy to make too: Sauté chopped asparagus with olive oil and some pressed garlic, add the juice of half a lemon and a couple of tablespoons of cream (adjust the creaminess by deciding how many tablespoons you want to add), then toss in some cooked linguine and mix it all, adding lemon zest! Trust me, it's so good!

STANIS'S TIP:
Remind yourself how important you are by buying yourself some cute flowers to adorn your living room, bedroom, garden, or balcony. I do it whenever I need a little pick-me-up, and trust me, spring will feel even more special!

MIAO
RECORDS
WELCOME!
BENVENUTI!
BLUES
DISCO
JAZZ
MEOW
BLUES
DINNER JAZZ
90s ROCK
70s ROCK
MEOW RECORDS
@stamisthecat

GROOVIN' WITH STANIS:
MY MUSIC COLLECTION

Jazz, soul, or swing—as long as I can listen to my favorite music, I'm happy. Jazz accompanies me constantly, and I have made my very own playlist, selected with my ears! These are my ten super favorite tracks to feel better!

- Ella Fitzgerald – "Walking in the Sunshine"
- Artie Shaw – "Non Stop Flight"
- Red Prysock – "Charleston Twist"
- Sonny Stitt – "Lester Leaps In"
- Miles Davis – "Will You Still Be Mine?"
- Peggy Lee – "Sweet Happy Life"
- Duke Ellington, Coleman Hawkins – "Limbo Jazz"
- Leo Park – "The Lion's Roar"
- Ella Fitzgerald – "Isn't This A Lovely Day?"
- Thelonious Monk, Sonny Rollins – "I Want to Be Happy"
- Benny Goodman, Helen Forrest – "Busy as A Bee (I'm Buzz, Buzz, Buzzin')"

@stanisthecat

Pawsitively Productive:
Stanis's Fun Home Chores

Cleaning the house? It has never been more fun!

Remo and Ottavia help me a lot when cleaning; being my two airborne friends (a pigeon and a seagull), their flying ability makes them very fast with many chores (they remove the dust from where I can't reach, for example!), and with them we came up with some fun and light solutions to make your cleaning days brighter and super fun!

Music! Music truly helps sync your body and your mind, and it creates a purrfect background for daily activities. When cleaning, I always opt for some good ol' funk! Groovy tunes are the purrfect ones for when you're sweeping the floor or doing the dishes, because you won't realize it, but you'll find yourself dancing! My tail is always keeping the pace of the song I'm listening to!

Do something you like right after! Set it as a prize. Allow yourself to look forward to it, and the chore will fly by! Eat something you really like or watch a video you saved a few days ago that you haven't had the time to watch yet, for example. As long as it is something that makes you feel good, reward yourself with it! I love to clean the house, but I'm not a big fan of the vacuum (my feline friends will understand), so I listen to music with my headphones. Immediately after, do you know what I do to make it all better? I, of course, eat a little tuna treat!

Buy colorful cleaning supplies, like sponges, brooms, and cloths, the more colorful the better! They will make your cleaning routine brighter and happier, and that's why I always try to buy dusters with prints on them! Paw prints are my favorite—could you have guessed?

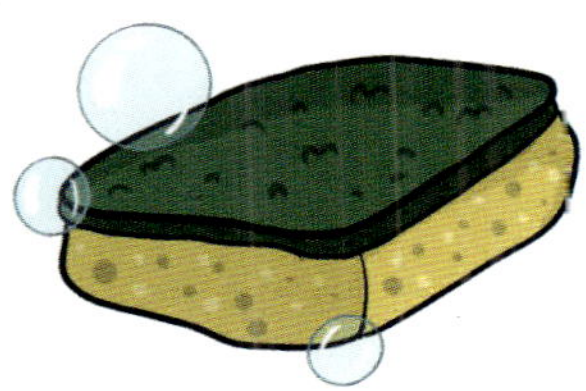

50

SUMMER VIBES WITH STANIS

What do I do during the summer? Oh, so many wonderful things! Whether I'm alone or with my friends, I make the most of the long, sunny days however I can.

While I, being a cat, do not cover myself in sunscreen, I always make sure I have some sun protection, be it a wide-brimmed hat, an umbrella, or a shawl. Then I pick a nice spot on my terrace (or balcony, garden, park, wherever you might like), lay out a picnic blanket, grab a book and a fresh drink, and **enjoy a good session of sunbathing**. Of course, I then seek the shade, which is the *purrfect* way to stay cool and comfy!

I love summer recipes, so I **make lots of tasty, summery treats** for me and my friends! I love pasta salads and fresh fruit (watermelon anyone?). I try to avoid using the oven if it's too hot outside (maybe the air fryer, but only if I have to).

Summertime is also for playing **sports**! I like soccer, volleyball, and tennis, and I challenge myself by playing it with Cesare (he's a sports fanatic!). One day I'll go to the Olympics, I know it! But I also **nap a lot**, especially when the weather gets a little too intense. I turn on a fan and enjoy the breeze as I snooze . . .

Corinna and I love to **host barbecues** (you can read more about how we organize our own on page 129). We love to share beautiful moments together with friends right before sunset, when the heat fades away and a gentle breeze starts to envelop us.

STANIS'S TIP: When it's too hot to nap but you still want to relax while lying down, grab a book of crosswords or word puzzles! That is how I like to enjoy a peaceful break! Then if you doze off after a few pages, just enjoy it!

@stanisthecat

Stanis's Painting and Drawing Tips

I'm an artsy little cat, and I *love* making art, both to hang around the house and to gift to my friends. Some of my art doesn't come out exactly how I imagined, but I'm so happy just to dive into the project. There's something special about moving my little paws around with colors and giving life to something!

Alcohol Markers: These are easy to use and purrfect for coloring! I use them all the time on very thick paper since they tend to bleed through. What's great about these markers is that they keep the color consistent without lines or spots, so it almost looks printed!

Oil Pastels: With these, my paws get dirty, and my creativity gets going! Oil pastels are purrfect for those afternoons when your creativity needs a boost. With these, I like to create simple drawings of food, fruit, and other objects. To blend the colors, use a bit of oil (applied with a little cloth, or your paws will turn every color imaginable).

Acrylic Paint: I love how bright and full acrylic paint is! Acrylics are quite easy if you're just starting, as they dry rather quickly and they maintain a lovely thick, full color. You can even paint over it without messing up the colors. Use acrylics on canvas for best results!

Watercolors: I'm not the best at watercolor, as this technique requires practice, but I can't help but try and try again. I might leave spots here and there and make the paper a little bumpy with the water running wherever it likes, but that's part of the fun!

Pencil Drawing: I always carry a little sketchbook and pencil with me, because you never know when your creativity might come knocking! You don't have to be an artist or a professional to feel like drawing. Challenge yourself and bring your pencil to the city or out in nature and start some landscaping sketches!

Fineliners: My favorite! When I hold fineliners, my ideas flow naturally, and I have discovered why: because it's a medium that doesn't scare me! They come in all sizes, from superthin to brush tip, and they are purrfect for doodling and scribbling. I keep a little notebook in which I just fill the pages with many little drawings (especially when I'm on the MeowPhone or waiting somewhere), and it's so fun to flip through and see them later!

WORKING FROM HOME, MY PAWSOME ROUTINE

I love to work smarter, not harder! It can, however, get a little tricky to stick with a routine that allows you to enjoy and work with a nice flow. As a cat, I know exactly how sometimes working from home can lead to many naps (oops), or to procrastinating a little, and there's absolutely nothing wrong with that of course! That's why I purrfected a wonderful routine to create a soft but effective workflow and came up with some tips that will make your working day real purrfect!

Start as early as you can. If you have tasks that need some attention before a call, take care of those early or before your official shift begins. Being awake extra early in the morning allows you to be super fresh (after your coffee, of course) and to have a mindful and more attentive outlook on what you'll work on! That's why I start my shift with coffee and lots of early morning zoomies!

Snacks and naps are very welcome! It can get a little overwhelming during your shift, but don't forget that the couch is just few steps away! Take a little restoring nap (put your alarm on to make sure you don't fall into deep sleep) and then have a nice smoothie to recharge! Snacks are the greatest (and yummiest) excuse to take a break, but don't forget to eat your main meals of the day too!

Choose the place where you'll be working that day. Is it your bedroom, your home office, or just the living room? Maybe try the garden or even a balcony, as long as it works for you! As a good cat, I love spots with lots of sun that allow me to enjoy the warmth and to work with natural light! Pick your place based on comfort and light, and make sure it's a spot without distractions or loud noises.

Have a schedule, but don't be too strict with it. If you feel like starting the day going out for breakfast or for a bike ride, allow yourself to do something pleasurable before your shift. Even if you start an hour or two later, your mood will thank you and your workflow will be extraordinary. Trust me, I know!

STANIS'S QUICK TIPS

- Listen to music if that helps you focus.
- If you're uncomfortable, use pillows for your posture and your neck.
- Make sure to get fresh air—take a walk and enjoy the outdoors to feel regenerated!

@stanisthecat
ART
GATTI
ROMA
STANIS' photos
ITALY

GARDEN
GREEN
PAW

Stanis at the Garden Center

Green leaves, colorful petals, and a fragrant smell all around: Welcome to the garden center, one of my favorite places in the world! Coming here is a ritual of mine; it helps me feel a little calmer and appreciate the beauty plants can hold. I spend a lot of time waltzing from one pot to another: lemon trees, roses, daisies (my favorites), and succulents too. We could all learn from succulents—they are cute and chubby but at the same time super strong and resilient!

So, you see me, with my little cart and my "Green Paw" tote bag, sauntering while grabbing new treasures for my terrace and collecting terra-cotta pots as well! When Remo accompanies me, he loves to help me around, and we play a few games, which makes our visit to the garden center super exciting! We love to say hi to the plants and make up silly names, so we walk by Lady Lavender or Sir Prickle the Cactus! We do scavenger hunts based on colors, too, during which we try to look for all the flowers that are pink or red or magenta—or to make it a little more challenging, we choose a color like indigo or butter yellow. So entertaining!

I buy plenty of cute flowers, especially for Corinna! She has a little balcony at her apartment, and she loves to decorate it with vibrant colors, so I pick the best ones for her. Her favorite? Pansies! They are a little difficult to plant and take care of, but I make sure to gift her a lovely bouquet of tulips and then some more, like gardenias!

The cats working at the garden center are honestly the best! They help you choose, understand, and pick the right plant, which is purrfect even for the cats that aren't very familiar with the plant's environment or needs. Taking care of them isn't the easiest thing, but I found out a little trick that, I don't know if it really works, but it makes my heart full: Speak with the plants any chance you get. My basil smells amazing and looks even better because I take the time to tell him that he is beautiful! That and water!

Stanis
NEW ON CATFLIX
UNDER COVER CAT
MEOWSTER Chef
THE REAL HOUSE CAT
TOP PICKS FOR YOU
PURRCESSION
GAME of PAWS
SATURDAY NIGHT LIVE
SILENT PAWS
PAW & ORDER
the clawffice
CATFLIX
MENU
VEG BISTROT
TAKE AWAY
@stanisthecat

Stanis's Favorite Rainy Day Activities

There's nothing better than being cozy at home while it's raining outside! As a cat, I love to curl up and nap, but I also love to keep myself busy and engaged in activities that are the purrfect pairing with a rainy day!

Collage

Grab old magazines, newspaper, and anything you might have at paw that has lots of images! Even supermarket ads, old phone books, or catalogs. Cut out all the images and text and pile them up in a box, grab glue, a scrapbook, or an album with thick paper, and start creating your stunning pieces. I love to make mine using cute stickers as well!

Tea and Movies

A blanket, a warm cup of your favorite tea, and an exciting new movie—sounds like a purrfect Stanis plan! I could curl up on my favorite spot on my couch and do this every day! The movies that warm my heart and brighten my day (even if it's gray outside) always star cats, obviously, and my favorite is *Kedi*, together with *A Street Cat Named Bob* and *The Garfield Movie*.

Miniatures

My itty-bitty paws are purrfect for my newest hobby: miniatures. There are miniature kits of every kind and place: bakeries, libraries, shops, and don't get me started about book nooks! I spend lots of time creating these little treasures; sometimes the result is a little crooked, but they are purrfect like that! It's challenging, but it makes me feel very proud.

Lego Building

I discovered these colorful bricks when I was a little kitty! I stepped on a few and thought, *Ow! These really hurt,* but I was also fascinated by how many wonderful things you could build with them! Since then, I love to either buy the cutest sets or use my loose pieces and build freely, letting my creativity flow! My last creation was a supercool bowl to put my keys in when I come home. So unique!

Stanis and Corinna
Date Ideas

When it comes to romance, yours truly can be quite excellent! Corina and I love to travel, explore, take walks, and just enjoy our time together as much as we can, because being with your loved one is just the best! If you don't have one yet, don't despair—it'll come soon. In the meantime, take notes!

Bike Rides and Sweet Treats

So imagine, it's a wonderful day and the weather is just purrfect. What to do, what to do . . . but of course! Let's go on a bike ride! Water, bells, helmets, and a lot of fun ahead. Time to go! Through a park, in the city center, or in the countryside, biking is fun and makes your paws go and your muscles work. After all that sport, something yummy to eat is mandatory, and sweet is the way to go! A lovely pastry or a refreshing ice cream, or maybe both, will let you two lovey-doveys end the date in the most delightful way.

Botanical Gardens

Amid hundreds of plants and flowers, your love will blossom even more! Grab a camera and head off to your local botanical garden, paw in paw. Through a rock garden or tropical greenhouse, lose yourself in one of the most magical places your city has to offer, stepping into beautiful and super-interesting nature. A purrfect date for those who like to take scenic walks!

Sunset Picnic

Oh, how romantic is the sunset? Even just enjoying it on your own! The sunset is magical and offers the purrfect background for a lovely picnic with yummy treats. A nice beach blanket, some sandwiches (my favorites are the one with cucumber and cream cheese), a bottle of rosé wine (I really love orange wine as well!), and olives to nibble on, of course! Then let the sky do its job! The light, the cuddles, and the food—can you ask for a better setting?

Pizzeria Date

Well, I'm an Italian cat, and so a romantic date at the pizzeria is a must! Margherita pizza with arugula, onions, and olives for me, thanks! I do love to pair a bruschetta with it and some fried deliciousness, such as *supplì* (fried mozzarella-stuffed rice balls with tomato sauce) and *fiori di zucca* (fried zucchini flowers filled with mozzarella and anchovies), to share with Corinna. Book an evening dinner at the coziest pizzeria in your city, dress up, and make it fancy! You don't need luxury or super-elegant restaurants for a glittery date!

PIZZERIA
PIZZERIA ROMANA
SUPPLÌ AL TELEFONO
PIZZA MARGHERITA
CROCCHETTE
BRUSCHETTE
e tanto altro!
VINO

Disclaimer: Not all flowers are safe for our furry friends.
Please research the plants you use, and exercise caution.

STANIS THE FLORIST: ASSEMBLING WONDERFUL BOUQUETS

When my day feels a little flat and I feel like I need some color in my life, there is one place that makes my heart full: the flower shop! I cast myself as a flower designer and buy everything I need to make wonderful bouquets for my house or to gift to my friends. There are so many styles for inspiration, shapes and sizes you can create, and colors to combine—fun doesn't even begin to describe it!

First, **get lost in the colors** and **choose a few striking flowers** (like roses, Gerbera daisies, Lisianthus, or sunflowers, which will serve as the main characters of the bouquet, as well as support flowers (like carnations or baby's breath). Build depth and vibrance, complementing the focal point flowers and adding texture with greenery, for example. I love ivy or fern, or you can even add an amazing scent with salal (lemon leaf)!

Make sure the flowers are fresh and to remove any foliage on the end of the stem. When it comes to **cutting the stem**, always do it at an angle, and **don't forget to remove any thorns**, ouch!

Now, **make a flowery sandwich**: greenery first, then the main characters, and then the supporting act! Decide the width and the length while working with your flowers and greenery: You can make it small and chunky for short, sturdy, and rustic vases, or lean for those classy flute-ish ones. Use wire or twine to secure the bouquet, and if it's a gift, make sure to use a lovely colorful ribbon. Don't forget to add a card to make it absolutely purrfect!

STANIS'S TIP: Change the water every day, and cut an inch or a few centimeters off of the stems to prolong the life of your stunning creation!

STANIS
STANIS music
Photos
Recipes
COOKIES
TRAVEL
ART
JAZZ
THE MYSTERY of the MIDNIGHT PURR

MY PURRFECT AUTUMN AFTERNOON

Leaves are falling, the sun is setting earlier, and the cups of tea are steaming. It can only mean one thing . . . it's autumn! Oh, how I love fall. I can't even begin to describe it, with its alluring atmosphere and the many cozy activities you can do; it's just purrfect. I have purrfected my very own autumn-y afternoon routine, which varies based on what I feel like doing. Coziness is around the corner—let's go!

When I'm in the mood for something super extra cozy, of course I grab my blanket, and I just curl up on the couch **watching movies with a cup of tea in my paws**. I love me some mint tea or a sweet cinnamon vanilla, and don't forget the cookies (with chocolate chips, please!).

If it's raining, I lean into my mysterious nature! The stormy weather calls for spooky stories, so **I grab a book and dive in** with the wonderful background noise of the thunder. Just purrfection! Accompany it with cookies and tea, obviously (you'll always find them around if I'm home during autumn!), along with some very low-volume instrumental jazz.

It smells amazing, and do you want to know why? Because **I just baked something delicious**! A pie or a batch of cupcakes—during the gloomy-but-wonderful days of autumn, you can find me wearing my apron, creating all sorts of scrumptious sweets. Cookies and tiramisu are my best recipes, which you can find in this book! Join me in a lovely baking session!

Autumnal afternoons are even better with friends! We **play many board games** and have lots of **TV series marathons** (snacks included, of course!). When I feel like I want to stomp my paws and crush some leaves, Remo and I go **book shopping,** or Corinna and I love to go for **afternoon walks** to get hot chocolates, cookies, doughnuts, and various pastries!

In the end, the purrfect autumn afternoon is the one that makes you feel cozy and fuzzy inside (in my case, also outside, thanks to my fur, which gets quite thick during the colder months). So enjoy autumn with anything that warms your heart, and always include some cookies—you can never go wrong!

HAPPY HALLOWEEN
TRICK OR TREAT?

Stanis loves Halloween!

Boo! It's spooky o'clock! I'm a black cat, so I consider Halloween to be my own holiday, the one that celebrates me and my fellow shadowy friends! Super scary or not, when the 31st of October hits, you'll find me ready for some fun!

I decorate everything, and when I say everything, I mean it! From the terrace to the foyer, my whole house becomes a haunted mansion, and my friends love it! Big spiders crawling on the walls (I'm a little afraid of them, but during Halloween, they become my best friends), spiderwebs hanging around, lanterns, and pumpkins in every corner. Pretty spooky, right?

I even prepare themed snacks, like cookies in the shape of ghosts and pumpkins, and "ghost" strawberries dipped in white chocolate, turned upside down and with the addition of googly eyes; they're so cute! Obviously, I stock up with all the candies in the world! Some years I love to stay at home and wait for all the kittens coming to trick-or-treat, while other times I have fun going around with my friends, doing it myself! You're never too old for moments of sweet fun!

The sun sets, and with it, darkness comes. That's when Halloween starts to take another shape, and so it's time for mysterious movies! Dimmed lights, candles lit, snacks within paw's reach, and the atmosphere is set! Halloween movie night is about to begin!

STANIS'S FAVORITE HALLOWEEN MOVIES:

- *Ghostbusters*
- *Casper*
- *The Nightmare Before Christmas*
- *Hocus Pocus*
- *Sleepy Hollow*

STANIS'S "AUTUMN BINGO"
FOR THE BEST FALL ACTIVITIES

For me, everything becomes magical when summer turns to autumn! Leaves change their colors, the air is crisp, and you can smell the spiced pastries from bakeries when you go on a walk! I love to enjoy this time of year exploring outside (but, hey, I love to loaf at home, as well, curling up and being at my coziest on my tiny red sofa!).

That's why I wrote this list of heartwarming activities, which you can do with me (I even put a little square close next to each idea, so you can check them off and make a fun autumnal challenge)!

- [ ] Drink herbal tea
- [ ] Take photos of the foliage
- [ ] Pick leaves for a nice collage or scrapbook
- [ ] Drink a cat-puccino while walking through the park
- [ ] Visit a pumpkin patch
- [ ] Buy a book and read it at home while snuggled in a blanket
- [ ] Hike somewhere beautiful
- [ ] Enjoy the smell of a fireplace
- [ ] Bake cookies and desserts in the morning
- [ ] Have soup and bread for dinner
- [ ] Bird-watch
- [ ] Drink warm apple cider
- [ ] Eat cinnamon buns and pumpkin bread
- [ ] Watch a spooky series with tea and cookies
- [ ] Enjoy the cool breeze
- [ ] Pick chestnuts
- [ ] Collect pinecones to use as decor in the house
- [ ] Watch the rain (or dance in it!)
- [ ] Wear plushy slippers
- [ ] Drink mulled wine

Christmas

STANIS CELEBRATES THE HOLIDAYS

Hello, Christmas! Twinkling lights, the smell of oven-baked lasagna, the clink of cutlery during a big lunch, the paper crunching when unwrapping gifts . . . I could go on for hours. Can you tell that I love Christmas so much?

Family and friends gather to celebrate and create new memories! My favorite part of the holiday season is without a doubt decorating and making sure that the atmosphere is purrfect! Corinna and I decorate the tree with the help of all our friends. Remo and Ottavia fly ornaments to the top of the tree to ensure there are no empty spots (fun fact: when you friends are birds, you don't need stepladders!). Meanwhile, we let our cookies bake in the oven, giving the house the best smell there is!

Then we place twinkling lights almost everywhere! The house has to feel extra cozy, of course, and so we make little snowballs, and we set cute miniatures around to add the extra touch I need for when I'm sipping my hot chocolate and I want to admire all the decor!

The holidays are also for super-delicious food! I make sure to create amazing menus for my guests (in this book, you can find some of my favorite festive bites and my special vegan Christmas cookies!).

I love to browse Christmas markets while drinking mulled wine and picking beautiful ornaments, but, hey, I DIY too! I love to make wreaths and homemade greeting cards in those cozy afternoons that precede the big day.

Celebrating together and spending valuable time with your loved ones is the most important part! Surrounded by love and warmth, the holidays go by very quickly, but they always leave a mark in your heart.

Make sure to celebrate and have fun with your family and friends this year! I like to think that you'll be celebrating with me and my friends too! *Auguri!*

SECOND
HAND
TREASURES
3€
20€
ART
2€
STORIA

Stanis's Marvelous Day at the Secondhand Shop

Let's go thrifting! I have my tote bag with me, my little wallet ready for action, and lots of excitement. I'm ready to dig deep with my paw through clothes, books, and little trinkets!

When I visit a flea market, I always get excited, as I know that I should be able to find amazing things at a very cheap price (well, sometimes; you need to be lucky!). My main interests are books and curious objects, especially when they're nice and dusty!

Another passion of mine that goes very well with secondhand markets is photography! I have my MeowPhone with me all the time and, of course, my phone's gallery is quite full. That's why I also bring a digital or analog camera wherever I go. Markets and secondhand shops always have these, and I love to lose myself admiring all the different types of cameras! One time, I found an analog camera at my local shop for €1 (I was purring with happiness!) and, despite its low price, it worked wonderfully. I still use it to this day!

Corinna, who always comes with me, loves to browse through cute clothes. She loves old-fashioned garments! I always tell her that we should organize a fun evening with our friends, all dressed like we're from the past.

Thanks to these special places, we can give a second life to tons of things. For example, an old camera or book that was just gathering dust is now in my little tote bag ready for action, and I couldn't love it more! Go visit your local thrift store and lose yourself in its fun maze of quirky and precious objects. It will be incredibly fun!

PURRSONAL PHILOSOPHIES

EAU DE PURRFUME
FOREST
MIST
@stanisthecat

WHAT CHEERS ME UP WHEN I'M BLUE

Sometimes our days can be a little grayer than usual, and that's okay! There are some days when I wish I could just curl up and sleep with lots of blankets on and purr all day. I also, however, like to color in those gray days with small, comforting, simple things that can be done from the coziness of my house.

Cook or bake, even if you're not good at it! Dirty your paws in the kitchen—have fun and experiment! If your morale is down, find a recipe you always wanted to make, get your coat on, head to the nearest market, and buy all the necessary ingredients. Wear an apron (or buy a fun one) and get to work! You'll find this not only amusing but super rewarding!

Take a hot shower or bath and wear your comfiest clothes! Take the time to pamper yourself with a long, hot shower (or bath) and wear the coziest lounge clothes you have. A shower always helps to clear your mind, and wearing something comfortable puts you at ease immediately. I always do this with my soft, cozy house robe (and if it's cold, I add a hot drink).

Read your favorite book! Whether you read it already or it's a new book waiting to be opened, read! Stories, words, and the turning of pages help you get in a positively focused mood, which will lull you into feeling better almost instantly. Do your reading in your favorite place in your home: the garden, living room, bedroom, or bathroom! For me, it's my cute little terrace, and if it's a little cold, I bring my blanket with me and enjoy it anyway!

"Pobody's Nerfect": Stanis's Solutions to Little Struggles

It's true, some days are tough. They can feel heavy and make us doubt everything! But at the end of the tunnel, there is always a flicker of light, helping us to see things in a different way.

We all struggle with something, big or small. From the moment we wake up to when we go to sleep, we all deal with our own battles. As I am a resilient little cat, I'll let you know my secret to combat this: Smile the moment you open your eyes in the morning. Meow loud and smile! That's one of my mottoes. Even if it doesn't feel like a smiling day, give it a try!

Sometimes, the world can feel like sand running fast through your paws, but as my sweet Corinna always says, "**You need to worry a little less about what you can't control**," with Remo adding, "**Stop worrying about things that aren't happening**." These two sentences always shift my days from cloudy to sunny.

What I truly believe, as cats are known to be very straight to the point, is that we—cats, humans, every species—are so amazing. Little fighters, dealing with so much every single day. It's so easy to get caught up in a big bubble of confusion. We forget to just smell the flowers and switch off the engine of negative thoughts.

When it hits you though, and you just can't bring yourself to lift a single toe bean about it, it's okay—don't be afraid to embrace it. We can learn so much! Plus, I've discovered that napping it out is a great solution as well!

STANIS'S PRACTICAL TIPS:

- Prioritize your needs and make time for things you really like and that distract you.
- Listen to some fun music, dance it out, go for an energetic run, move your body, and shake it.
- Get cozy, literally, and relax watching something or reading a beautiful book (like mine, for example).
- Learn to say no, limit negativity, and focus on the little positives, even if there are just a few.

Stanis
PLANTS DIAR
@stanisthecat

STANIS ON HOW TO EMBRACE THE CALM

Let's be honest: Some days aren't as great as we would love them to be. It can be very easy to feel overwhelmed, even with the tiniest things, and that can make us forget our need to slow down. But I've worked it out, so when you want to unplug and find your own precious peace of mind, my feline wisdom will give you a warm hug.

Life is just the best! I have to admit, though, sometimes it feels like a machine that never stops, with its engine getting warmer and warmer, louder and louder, and eventually needing a well-deserved rest in order to function! I, Stanis, embrace the calm by turning off that engine every time I can.

I put everything on pause, and I try to focus on enjoying life with my favorite little things: cooking, reading, drawing, and visiting family and friends.

Though it might seem a little silly, calmness is in the simple things. It hides in plain sight, and we very often just steer clear of it without knowing.

If you're having a difficult time, remind yourself that tough moments come and go. Sometimes they last a long time, sometimes a matter of days. In between those days, months, or even years, like a sandwich, don't forget to put slices of happiness.

THE FOUR RULES FOR EMBRACING THE CALM À LA STANIS:

- If you have a hobby you want to start, a sweet you want to eat, or a trip you want to go on, do exactly that! Happiness shouldn't be postponed.
- Sleep, eat, drink water, and pamper yourself. Think of yourself as a jewel that needs polishing every day.
- Take your time, think, and don't get angry. Sometimes it's not even worth it, so take a deep breath and turn the page to the next chapter.
- Unclench your jaw, drop your shoulders, and take deep breaths. You deserve it.

@stanisthecat

STANIS AND THE ART OF PROCRASTINATING

"Oh well, I'll do it later!" How many times have you said these words? Maybe not the exact same ones, but I know they ring a bell. But don't ever feel guilty! Doing things a little later than you planned is purrfectly normal, and dare I say, we should all do it more often.

First of all, we procrastinate not because we are lazy but because we feel like we have to. We need to make sure that all of our tasks and must-dos become choices instead of mandatory orders! Remember that you have all the freedom in the world; so, dear laundry, let's get you folded tomorrow!

Don't let the guilt creep up on you. When you feel like you want to postpone something, schedule it in advance or try to think of when you'll do it. You'll feel conscious of your choice, less guilty for not doing it yet, and happy because you can now think of doing something else (like a nap, for example).

Okay, now you've postponed something that you really don't want to do. Think of ways to fill up this time. You can avoid that task you really aren't in the mood for, but you should embrace a task you reeeaaally want to do now! A hobby, or an activity that gives you joy!

Write a minimal to-do list! Keep your procrastination organized and super simple to handle. Lazy, yes, but organized, à la Stanis!

Now, speaking of priorities: When I have a chance to take a nap, trust me, I never say I'll do it later!

Be happy,
purr a lot,
eat well
and
NAP zzz
DON'T FORGET TO SMILE

Stanis's Motivational Tips

Life, oh life, you are so cute and wonderful but sometimes very challenging. Yours truly has concocted a few gentle tips for feeling motivated and just, you know, not alone. So when it feels a little uncomfortable, just grab my book, read these tips, and take a big, deep breath. I'm pretty sure that they will help you—Stanis's word!

For When You Feel Low . . .

My main advice for when life gets a little tricky and brings you down is to do your favorite thing: Make yummy, comforting food, go out with friends and have fun, play some music, or create something beautiful with your paws! The choices are endless, really. I, for example, love to cook and whip up delicious dishes for me and my friends, read mysterious books or travel guides for future awesome trips, and just enjoy the breeze from my window.

For When You Feel Hopeless . . .

I have a motto that I repeat to myself whenever I feel a little down: "Tomorrow is going to be better, but I'll make today wonderful anyway!" You should always have some resilience in your pocket, ready to use, and I've learned that fighting through it with positivity is the way to go! You know what works for me? Writing down all my dreams, looking at them, and then asking myself, *Which one can I make real in the next few days?* It works every time!

For When You're Scared . . .

It's never easy to figure out what to do when life puts us at a crossroads, but I have learned another useful lesson: Don't be afraid. When you know the right thing to do, fear is just there to make you wonder whether you should do it, and that's not necessarily a bad thing. That feeling, though, should become the positive push. Fear should become the purrfect excuse to say, "Hey, you know what?! I'm ready!"

For When You Feel Lost . . .

Sometimes life feels like a maze, one that often decides to trick you and change directions. It can be confusing and tough, but it's important to remember that deep in our hearts, we are strong and beautiful. We know that even if the maze has changed, a little safe path to walk our paws on is always around the corner, even when we can't see it or we're too scared to proceed.

THE ART OF ENJOYING YOUR OWN COMPANY

When I think of my friends, my heart warms up! They are simply the best. They make me feel happy, and we can share lots of awesome adventures! I wouldn't change them for anything in the world. Sometimes, though, we are all busy and I find myself on my own, but it never gets lonely! On the contrary, spending time alone is super relaxing, and it allows me to dive deep into passions of mine.

WHAT DO I DO WHEN I'M ALONE?

I nap! Napping is one of my favorite things to do. Curling up for a nice restoring sleep is always a good idea, especially when you're a cat.

I cook and bake my favorite things. Cooking for yourself is a gentle act of love, and I always treat myself to something I really like.

I go out shopping! There's nothing better than to grab a couple of sweet treats at a bakery and walk around browsing shops.

I walk to the nearest garden center and admire all of their wonderful plants. My terrace is full of nice plants, and even if I will eventually start to run out of space, there's always room for one more!

I sip new flavors of tea. I like to buy and try different teas (during the winter my favorites are vanilla, cinnamon, and orange), and nothing goes better with tea than a nice book.

I catch up on TV shows and movies! I love to watch almost everything, from mysteries to documentaries. So I grab my blanket, a nice little snack, and I lose myself in a new, captivating series.

I journal daily! I have a little notebook in which I jot down my thoughts, describing my day. It's always nice to read past pages, as it helps me improve myself! It's a soothing habit that I look forward to each day. To make it fun, I even write with colorful pens and add pretty stickers.

I organize parts of my house, for example drawers, photo boxes, shelves, and bookcases. Finding old things while creating a new organized space helps me a lot, and it's truly so much of fun!

I dance and do silly things, like singing out loud with a hairbrush as a microphone! This always makes me super happy (I laugh a lot while doing it) and reminds me to be carefree and just embrace who I am!

ART
MEOW
RECIPES
Stanis
TODAY IT WAS A GOOD DAY!
Stanis

SELF-CARE WITH STANIS

VELVET PAWS
@stanisthecat

STANIS'S TIPS ON HOW TO HAVE A GOOD NIGHT'S SLEEP

Stretching and napping? You're talking to a pro! Curling up and preparing for a nap is one of our talents (I speak for all my fellow cats around the world!), but taking one for hours is undoubtedly our best! After some discussions with my feline friends, I have summed up four very useful tips for enjoying a good night's sleep and feeling restored **(like me, you might even wake up extra early for some good ol' zoomies!)**.

Pamper Yourself!

A long bath or a warm shower always does the trick. The warmth and the sound of water helps me relax, and it instantly makes me feel rested, which is a purrfect start for a good night's sleep. I also put a face mask on and use a jade roller on my face (Corinna suggested I use it, and it works wonders!) to make my routine a little fancier.

Drink Something Warm

An herbal brew is a great drink choice before curling up. I love chamomile; I've been drinking it since I was a little kitten, and the smell and taste already soothe me to sleep. I sometimes go for fresh mint, which helps digestion, especially after pizza night with my friends! There are so many infusions to choose from, and as long as you have something warm in your paws, you'll know that you'll get a superb sleep!

Stretch Your Body

Before every good nap, there's a stretching session—as a cat, I guarantee it! I love to stretch fifteen to twenty minutes before going to sleep; it helps me unwind and at the same time makes my body feel incredibly relaxed. You can either do some yoga positions (my favorite is, of course, cat pose, which helps stretch out my back when I've been working all day) or even just stretch as you please. Focus on whichever muscles are a little sore and tired after your day's activities, which will allow you to feel free and at ease!

Read a Book (and Put Down Your Phone)

The most important trick for sleeping like me (aka, a king) is to put away your phone at least one hour before sleeping. Scrolling, reading, or just watching videos on your phone doesn't help, as the light wakes you up and doesn't allow your body and mind to prepare to relax. Pick a book, instead, and put your phone on the charger (which will also help you to wake up immediately in the morning, as you need to get up to snooze your alarm!).

STANIS'S TIP: If you don't like to read, keep a little notebook close to your bed, and right before going to sleep, write down your thoughts, positive or negative. It's the purrfect way to empty your mind and get a good night's sleep.

Spa Day for Stanis

Filing my nails, getting pampered with massages, having a restoring quick nap or a nice session of fur-care—spa day is a must for me! I don't do it every day, as there are so many daily things to do, but I always make sure to dedicate some time at least once a month. Of course, spa day involves a lot of purring and eating too!

9:00 AM

Wake up and open your windows, cloudy or sunny, and let the light come in! Move on to the kitchen and whip up a yummy breakfast—yogurt with granola, toast with homemade jam, or some overnight oats. Try to keep it delicious but balanced.

9:30 AM

Grab a notebook and a pen (even some colorful ones, if you like) and list all the things you're grateful for, with details! For example, I'm incredibly grateful for my friends, nature, and my life (I'm a world-famous cat after all!), but I'm also grateful for daisies, rain, and the fact that I'm able to travel and discover this beautiful, fascinating world. Add some drawings and, while writing, listen to some light music.

10:30 AM

Time to stretch! Put on your favorite comfy pants, start moving your body like you would if you were an inflatable tube man, and just dance away. Have some fun! The sillier the movements the better! Then stretch your back and your legs, like we cats do, and go back to dancing.

11:00 AM

Did you sweat a little? Either way, it's time for a nice shower or bath! Use your favorite products, like bath salts or a bath bomb and fancy soap, and do it all! Smelling good, feeling fresh, and most importantly, keeping our fur shiny and soft is the key to feeling purrfectly lush!

11:30 AM

All the routines! Manicure (I normally scratch my nails on the couch, but you can use different tools, like a nail file or a nail cutter), fur-care (don't forget sunscreen, always!), and any other beauty routine you like. Take your time, just relax, and then look at the mirror: You look gorgeous!

12:30 AM

Time to eat! Let's do it healthy and appetizing: salad with fresh tomatoes, arugula, and a drizzle of olive oil, carrots with hummus, lentils with a sprinkle of salt, oil, and lemon juice, and some yummy multigrain bread to pair it with (this is my go-to lunch when I do my spa day!). Eat seasonal fruit, like apples or peaches, depending on the season.

MEOW BALM
Kitty Glow
PURRFECT SPA
VELVET PAWS
EAU DE PURRFUM
@stanisthecat

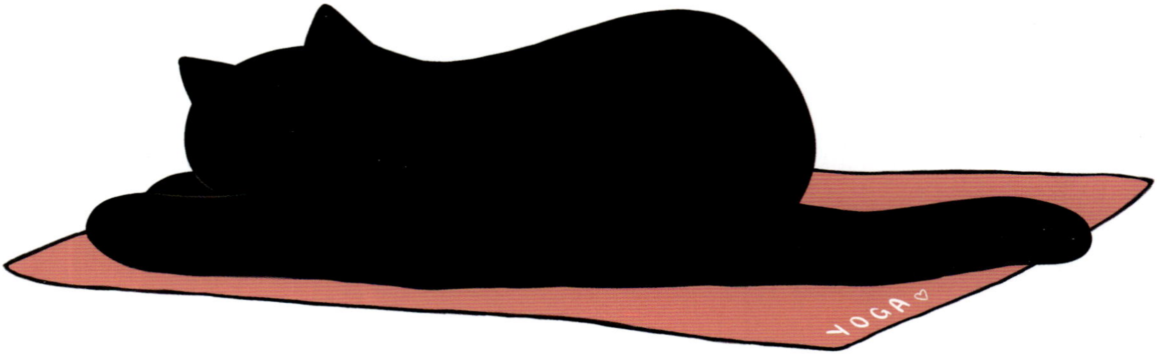

YOGA WITH STANIS

You know what fixes almost everything when you're feeling a little down? Pizza, of course! But I find that yoga is a good contender as well! Stretching my muscles and breathing deep are very important to feeling at ease, connected, and balanced. I've worked out a simple routine I do every day that helps me feel elastic, strong, and less stressed, which is very important!

Tree Pose

This pose helps me with my balance and improves my already purrfect stability.

Child's Pose

Relaxing and so comforting, this pose makes me feel very rested (sometimes I even fall asleep and take a short nap).

Downward Facing Dog (or Cat) Pose

This is probably every cat's favorite! It helps stretching your back, shoulders, legs, arms, and paws.

Mountain Pose

Ground your paws on your mat and enjoy the power of this pose, which helps you feel a little more rooted to the present.

Warrior Pose

Oh, I love this one! It makes me feel very powerful and strong. This position helps make your legs sturdier and opens your chest and hips.

STANIS'S TIPS FOR THE BEST YOGA SESSION: Put on some relaxing music, wear comfy clothes, and don't forget to do it barefoot (or barepaws, in my case). Use a soft mat that allows you to be comfortable when doing positions that require bending or lying down. Ultimately, focus on your breath and listen to your body. If some positions feel a little too tight or unnatural, allow yourself to modify them to suit your level of comfort.

@stanisthecat
TOMATOES

Stanis loves Nature

I'm a city cat, but deep down, I live in my cottage era every day! Nature is such a fundamental part of our lives: It nurtures us, and it makes us better cats. Whether you live in the city or in the countryside, here are a few ideas to tie yourself to nature a little more.

Growing and Tending

If you have a large patch of grass, you know what to do: Plant all the veggies! Maybe also some cute little fruit trees (I have a lemon tree and I love it). When living in the city, make sure to gather some balcony pots and planters and grow all the herbs you like, which are very easy to manage if you have a little space or just want something fresh out of your balcony or terrace in no time!

Let's Get Sporty!

Paws at work, let's move our bodies! When I go to my cottage, I love to follow the paths and explore fields—so relaxing! Forests are alsc so enchanting (just make sure to follow hiking trails to not get lost)! Parks, bike paths, and riversides do the job when in the city, and even the beach! Nature isn't just green leaves and mountains; I do love me some sea salt as well!

Animals, Our Little Friends

Spotting and encountering gentle friends is a favorite pastime of mine! Deer, foxes, and lots of birds (Remo knows so many of them, he is such a famous pigeon)—these animals are most likely to be seen in their natural habitat, and we always need to be very respectful of them. In the city? Oh well, that's where I met most of my friends, but you have the chance to spot ducks and squirrels as well! They are so fun!

Creativity Burst

It doesn't matter where I am; my creativity always flows. Whether in the countryside or in the city, there are tons of ways to engage with nature and art. Photography, for example, or painting in a tranquil setting by the lake, or even some urban sketching in a lovely old *piazza*. Just make sure to bring what you need, even just a pencil and a notebook, and to have fun.

STANIS'S TIP: Try the universal activity when it comes to enjoying food in nature: picnic! Under a tree, in the middle of a field, by a lake, or in a city park, it's always a good time for some good ol' picnicking! Prepare some sandwiches (cream cheese and cucumber are my go-to), some fresh fruit, some snacks like olives or breadsticks, and a fruity lemonade! So purrfect!

Stanis Makes Candles!

Who doesn't like to light candles to make their space a little cozier and more sparkly? I have a weakness for them: Scented or with curious shapes, in glass jars or simple tea lights, candles are an absolute must in my house. I use them for every occasion, especially when I want my space to become a little more comfy and warm.

As I buy so many, I have even learned to make my own! It is such a relaxing and calm pastime; I can't stop now that I know how fun it is. Using soy instead of beeswax (because bees are my friends), I make candles using essential oils to scent my home exactly how I like, especially vanilla and fragrant smells like freshly baked cookies or even tomato sauce (no, I'm joking—but wouldn't that be a great candle scent?). Let me give you some tips on how to approach your candle-making sessions.

What You Need

The Basics: soy wax, a container that will serve as the mold for your candle, candle wicks with holders, a thermometer, a tool for stirring, two pots and water to make a double boiler for melting wax, and scissors.
Add-ons: essential oils and dye to make your candles colorful!

Disclaimer: Furry readers should leave this activity to their human companions.

How to Make

It might scare you at first, but making candles is easier than you think! Prepare your workspace and melt the wax by heating it in your double boiler. Making sure to stir, add your essential oils or fragrances and dye while the wax is still hot to allow an even distribution. Pour the wax in the container you've chosen and secure the wick, which needs to be placed before pouring. The wick needs to be centered and as straight as possible so your candle will melt evenly when you light it. The candle needs to fully rest until hardened, then just trim the wick and enjoy the coziness you have created!

STANIS'S TIP: Experiment with different combinations of essential oils to create your very own signature scent! Vanilla and cinnamon or lavender and mint, the world of scents is within paw's reach!

DETECTIVE CAT

Stanis's Tips for Sick Days with the Cold or Flu

Oh no! You got sick? That can be the worst, I know. Your nose is running, you're cold and then you're warm, and you wish you could just snap your toe beans and feel healthy again. No matter the season, getting sick is never fun. When my friends are sick, I use these little tips to help; each is full of love, a very important ingredient in healing.

Staying cozy is the key, so if you don't stay warm with lots of blankets (purring like I would), then what are you doing?! Go get your comfiest pajamas, warmest socks, and fuzziest blanket. If you need to get up, do like I always do and walk around with your blanket like a cape. You'll look very royal or like a superhero, and you'll keep warm!

Staying hydrated is super important to keep in mind when you're feeling under the weather. It helps replenish your energy. Water, hot soups, juices, and smoothies full of vitamins will do the trick. I always think that a warm bowl of soup when feeling ill brings you halfway to recovery already (and by the way, check my recipe on page 135 for my special soup for when you're feeling sick; it's like a magic potion!).

Sleep as much as you can! As a cat who naps endlessly, I can't meow loud enough about how good sleep is for everything. Feeling sick? Sleep, and you'll recover in no time. Angry with the world? Sleep, and your body will wake up a little more relaxed. So curl up, get cozy, and doze off for as long as you need.

Make sure to surround yourself with people who can take care of you if needed! You are strong every day, but asking for help once in a while is okay, even if it's just for a chat or some company.

SWEATERS
M
Vintage PAWS
SHOP
CLOTHES, ACCESSORIES, DECOR & MORE
NEW COLLECTION
PURRFECTLY VINTAGE
Stanis the cat
2€ HATS

STANIS'S COZY WARDROBE FOR THE CHILLY MONTHS

Oh, how much I love the crisp days, when you need to cozy up with layers! I have an extensive collection of sweaters (my red one is my favorite), and I show off so many of them during Christmas! But, of course, I love me some stripes, as well (they say that horizontal ones make you look slightly larger, but I'm very proud of my round size, so it doesn't matter to me), and fall-themed sweaters with leaves, chestnuts, and warm colors.

Inside my closet, you can find lots of mittens. My little paws get cold very quickly during winter, so I prepare myself with lots of colorful mittens that I can interchange whenever I want and, most importantly, pair with my outfit. I sometimes even knit them, as they are very easy to make (they don't have fingers!).

I don't wear berets a lot, but when I do, they have to be special. I bought and wore one in Paris when I visited with Corinna, and that one is a precious part of my collection! I love earmuffs, as you probably can imagine: They keep my cute little triangles warm and cozy.

I must mention my favorite items: scarves! Well, I just have one, my iconic red scarf, which keeps me warm wherever I go. The cool thing about scarves is that you can tie them any way you prefer. For example, Corinna makes a cute little knot in front, and I like to wear my scarf a little loose in a way that falls down my back (very chic, in Corinna's words).

I shop most of my items at Vintage Paws, the vintage shop Corinna runs, as I love to be sustainable and reuse old clothing that needs some renewed love. Finding sizes is a little hard sometimes, but that's part of the fun!

STANIS'S TIP: When it's really, really cold, or I visit somewhere pretty chilly, I love to wear a thermal shirt, which allows me to feel warm and creates a layer of extra coziness.

TRAVEL TALES

@stanisthecat
TO DO
LUGGAGE
PASSPORT
CHECK-IN
MIAO AIRLINES
Stanis
TO DO
Map

Stanis's Luggage: What I Always Bring with Me on My Trips

Traveling is so exciting, isn't it? You get to discover so much, see amazing things, meet wonderful people (and cats!), and learn lots of new things you'll carry in your heart—and in your luggage! My luggage is a little messy (don't you worry) but always organized, and I make sure to never forget my travel essentials.

My camera is a must! I love to use a film camera because you don't get to see your shots right away—it's so exciting! Disposable ones are handy, especially if it is your first time. I also use my MeowPhone, and a little digital camera as a backup, just in case I run out of film or battery. When traveling, remember to tie a little strap on your camera so it's easy to carry.

Your most important things, such as your **passport**, **visa** (if necessary), and **boarding pass** should be within paw's reach. Either digital or physical, triple-check before leaving your house! I always double-check everything, but the triple check when traveling is a must.

Wallet, cash, and cards: Never forget the trio! To make sure you remember it the day you're leaving, place all the necessary items right next to the door, and maybe add a sticky note that says, *Hey, don't forget these!* It's so easy to forget things when we are excited or in a rush.

Traveling has to be comfy, of course! So prepare everything you might need in order to feel good and cozy: **neck pillow, face mist, earplugs, comfy shoes, some snacks, and water**.

For strolling around your destination, keep in your bag some **wet wipes, sunscreen** (to apply every couple of hours), **some bandages for blisters, hand sanitizer, and tissues**. These basics are a must, and you will be glad to know you're covered!

Regarding **clothes**, pack your luggage based on your destination, research the rules and how the weather will be, and try to keep it light (it gives you the chance to buy some unique clothes when you're visiting).

STANIS'S MUST-HAVES:
MeowPhone and its power bank, guidebook, cameras, sunscreen, and a desire to explore (make sure you have tons of that!).

I ♥ LONDON
Stanis

9:00 NEW YORK
9:30 BERLIN
9:45 LONDON
10:10 PARIS
10:20 LISBON
11:00 PRAGUE
11:15 BARCELONA
MEOW AIRLINES
@stanisthecat

Stanis at the Airport

It's travel o'clock! Luggage? Done! Boarding passes? Done! Now, I'm finally at the airport and I can enjoy my trip! But what is there to do at the airport? Lots, of course! I know that waiting for a flight can be tiring, but it can also be very exciting.

For example, I just can't get enough of **crosswords** and **puzzle books**; solving puzzles and thinking with a pencil in my paw helps the time pass by quickly. Even if I don't feel like doing it at the start, as I could probably take a nap or scroll on my MeowPhone, I focus on it and start to have lots and lots of fun!

If I'm with a friend, **Doodle Stories** is a game I invented (or maybe not, I'm not sure) that lots of you already know by another name. You only need a sheet of paper, two pencils, and a lot of creativity! The first player draws something and the other continues the drawing, adding to the one previously made. You can create battles and cute or quirky stories, and you can add dialogue as well! It will make your time at the gate fly by—literally.

It's never a bad time for **music**! My jazz playlist (which you can find on page 29) is my go-to for everything. It relaxes me and gives me a serotonin boost! Most of all, it makes me energized to explore my destination and creates a lovely soundtrack for the trip! That's why before every trip I take, I add a new song to my playlist, creating a wonderful memory for the next time I hear it.

MEOW SPF
50
TUNA treats
Stanis
Stanis
What's in my bag?
-Stanis-

WHAT'S IN MY BAG?

When I stroll around, an essential must-have is my tote bag! I collect so many of them (I have a tote bag for every occasion!) and they are so comfortable and super useful to bring everything with you!

In mine, for example, you'll find:

My little sketchbook (and pencil) for thoughts and sketches. It's very handy. When you write or draw things down, it helps clear your head!

Sun protection! Because it's very important to care about your skin and fur, obviously. The sun is warm and makes days beautiful, but we need to be careful and apply protection (shawls, wide-brimmed hats, or sunscreen for my furless friends) all the time!

My little coin purse, which contains all my money! Also, the pattern on the coin purse matches my favorite blanket during the colder months!

Of course, **tuna treats**! I love tuna, and I can't go out without my favorite snacks. They give me energy throughout the day, and it's always nice to treat yourself with a little tasty bite.

My **MeowPhone**! To keep up with trends and discover new music but also to chat with my friends and to send emails for work. I really like to take photos with it—it relaxes me and makes me happy browsing my gallery full of nice memories!

A **Polaroid picture** of a very wonderful sunset from my terrace!

My favorite toy! Which I bought more than seven years ago, but it still makes me happy, and I have so much fun with it! It doesn't matter if it's ruined or very old; some things are just your favorites and you wouldn't change them for anything in the world.

REMO
@stanisthecat
Stanis

Stanis Goes Hiking

Stepping my paws into nature is always the best! Be it wonderful forests, hidden grottos, historical paths, or just the calmness of Mother Nature, I can't resist exploring, and guess what? It helps me stay in shape and to keep my energy levels high! I gear up and off I go! But what really helps is the fact that I'm a cat. Aren't I the cousin of my friends the lion, panther, leopard, and company?

When I hike, I usually do it with my friends. We like to pick beautiful places and bring our cameras to capture everything we see. I don't bring a map because Remo brings one and checks the perimeter, telling us where to walk so we don't get lost! One piece of advice, though: If you don't have Remo with you, use your MeowPhone to check the route and to make sure to stay on track.

Bring a little snack like dried apple slices, my go-to when hiking, and don't forget to bring water and a little baggie for your garbage. It's always important to respect nature and not litter in these places full of magic. I usually am the guide of the group, and I love to tell my friends about nature, especially trees: Did you know that some of them can live for thousands of years, or that they can communicate with each other through soil?

I love to hike because that's when I collect leaves. It's one of my many favorite hobbies! I let the leaves dry and then place them with care in a scrapbook, dedicated to all the leaves I find when I go for beautiful walks. Leaves can be so wonderful with their stunning colors, from dark red to mustard yellow; some of them are so interesting with their quirky or harmonious shapes, too, and they're so worthy of being collected.

@stanisthecat

Stanis Takes the Train

Choo-choo, all aboard! Traveling by train is so fun and such a relaxing way to admire the views and take in the world a little slower. I'm a cat who loves to try lots of new things, and when I first tried the train when I was a little kitten, I couldn't help but love it immediately. Ever since, whenever there's a destination to reach by train, you'll find me excitedly jumping aboard!

On a sunny or rainy day, the window seat is just the best spot for getting lost in the sights. Countrysides, cities, or small rural areas—even the industrial or a little rough—the views from the train are always super interesting and full of rich scenery. **I love to sketch** the ones that capture my attention and add the date to create a special memory of that moment. If you have a long ride coming, sketching out the landscape is a good idea, as the trip will go much faster!

When I'm traveling with Corinna, Remo, Cesare, and Ottavia, we play games and spend the time in creative ways. We bring a set of **conversation cards**, or we play **Would You Rather?** with silly and sweet questions. For example, Remo loves to ask: "Would you rather eat one giant cookie or one hundred cupcakes?" and, "Would you rather get photobombed by a goose in every picture or be followed by a parade of ducklings?" He's so creative!

I also love to **watch a movie** when I travel solo, or I **edit all the photos I take with my MeowPhone** each day. It's relaxing, easy, and (despite spending time in front of the screen) I feel productive as I'm doing something for my creativity and my coziness, which are very important.

I travel by train because it's romantic and makes me feel like a vintage cat discovering the world in leisure. You know those fancy, wonderful trains with restaurants in their carriages? Oh, I love them! They always inspire me to write a mystery series in which I, Stanis, am the detective solving a case. I already know my catchphrase: "**Elementary, my dear Remo**."

@stanisthecat
STANIS'
TOMATO SAUC
NIS'
AUCE

MY COZY COTTAGE RETREAT

When I feel overwhelmed and I need to be in contact with nature, I like to retreat either with myself or with my friends to my cozy cottage in the countryside. Going there gives me all the wonderful feelings I need to recharge and feel like a new cat. The jasmine with its delicious and fragrant smell, my little pond filled with golden fish swimming around, and the vegetable garden I've built—this little corner of heaven is the purrfect spot for unwinding.

Corinna loves to decorate the garden during spring and summer, putting up little fairy lights around the trees, painting the terra-cotta pots in different colors so the flowers are even more vibrant, and buying all sorts of pretty tableware, from tablecloths to cups and cutlery. I love when we set the table for our evenings, especially since I get to make my own placeholder!

Remo often comes over to help me organize and maintain my cottage, as you can probably imagine that having a place surrounded by nature requires lots of care. He looks over the property to see if everything is okay, and then we set up a to-do list: removing the weeds, harvesting the fruit from the trees, cleaning up where needed, and making little fixes around the house. When things get a little difficult, Cesare comes to help, as well, and let me tell you, we make the best team!

I love to cook, and when I'm here, my imagination runs wild! With all the produce my garden offers, I usually make jams, sauces, and all sorts of preserves. Strawberry compote, lemon jam, and my super-delicious tomato sauce. With my jams and compotes, I make Linzer cookies and pies, and I always make sure to bring a couple of jars back so I can have the best breakfasts ever!

The sound of the birds singing, the leaves dancing with the wind, the sunny days (and the gloomy ones as well) give me so much energy. They offer exactly what every cat needs to feel tranquil, and so I curl up with my book or to take a nap, and I just let the nature and the calmness do their job.

@stanisthecat

STANIS GOES CAMPING!

Fun awaits, and I'm just so excited because it's time to go camping! Corinna, Remo, Cesare, and Ottavia are coming, too, and I just can't wait! Activities, nature, and quality time—camping helps us escape our stress for a little bit, thanks to the wonderful sights and outdoor activities!

When I go camping with my friends, I already know that I'm going to have a weekend full of amazing memories and lots of laughter! We set up a few tents, we bring sleeping bags, and we all share some chairs and tables. We keep it essential but very comfy! I take care of bringing the cooking equipment (I need to make my tomato sauce wherever I go; I'm practically famous when I cook outside of my house, as the smell always attracts willing taste testers) and, of course, packing snacks, water, and some canned food.

Remo brings the navigation tools and guides us together with Ottavia—they're specialists at that. Cesare and Corinna gather up the blankets and pillows, so we are all set for amazing adventures!

Putting up a tent is very fun but a bit complicated, so we always make sure to follow the instructions accurately. After that, we build a little fire for cooking and for staying warm during the evening. The real deal, though, starts right after: We play so many board games and card games, we hike through the wonderful paths and fields, and we enjoy our time together breathing the fresh air. I also get to read *a lot*—the sound of nature is the purrfect background for focusing! Hiking, playing games, exploring around, you name it! My friends and I do it all and make the most out of it, and at the end of the day, while roasting our marshmallows, it's so amazing to relive the day's events and share with others!

STANIS'S TOP ACTIVITIES WHEN CAMPING:

Stargazing: Saying hi to all the glittery stars before falling asleep is my favorite.

Swimming: I love a relaxing and refreshing swim (not all of us do, I know).

Campfire stories: Spooky or not, we tell so many tales when the sunset hits, and it's very magical.

Bird-watching: Remo and Ottavia do it, as well, as they encounter so many longtime friends.

MARVELOUS MEOWTHFULS

FRESH FRUIT & VEGGIES EVERYDAY!
PASTA WEEK! ♡
OPENING HOURS:
MONDAY - SATURDAY
9:00 - 19:30
MEOW MARKET ♡
MEOWY PRICES
POMODORI ♡ TOMATOES € 1,49 kg
FUSILLI
PASTA FUSILLI
FARFALLE
OLIO
FRESH TOMATO SAUCE
Stanis the cat

STANIS'S LIST FOR THE PURRFECT GROCERIES

Shopping for groceries is one of my favorite activities! I love to roam around the store looking for all the ingredients I need for my recipes. Sometimes it can be overwhelming, as there are so many options to choose from, but I've worked out a supersmart way of doing it that doesn't drain you too much!

Make a List in Advance

To avoid wandering for too long, prepare a list! If you have no plan for what you'll be purchasing, then opt for at least the sections you'll spend most of the time in. For example, do you know that you might need some fruit, some carbs, or frozen items but not exactly sure which? Write the sections down! That will help you navigate the store a little better.

Take Your Time

I know, we go very fast in this world, but I sometimes take the excuse of shopping for groceries as a moment to relax. I allow myself to just take a stroll, discovering new products or finding inspiration for a last-minute recipe. Allowing yourself to let this errand feel entertaining could really change your day!

Grab the Right Stuff!

Two important rules: Always check the expiration date and pick the freshest stuff! Normally, when I need to pick up veggies and fruit, I opt for the farmers market, which offers the best produce. For the rest, I rely on my little herb garden on my terrace and (of course) the supermarket or local delis around me. I like to chat with fellow vendor cats when I visit local shops!

What to Buy for Stanis-Approved Groceries

Chickpeas, lentils, and **broad beans** should always be in your cupboard, since they're purrfect for salads and delicious main dishes. **Tomato sauce**, of course, is a good one! **Spreads**, like olive tapenade, to spread on bread, are purrfect for an appetizer! **Pasta**—fusilli and spaghetti are my favorites! Speaking of **veggies**: tomatoes, cabbage, zucchini, onions, and carrots are my basics; you can come up with truly amazing dishes with them.

Stanis Loves Breakfast

When I wake up (very early, as my fellow cats know purrfectly well), the first thing to do is eat and energize myself for the day ahead! I love breakfast because I can choose from so many options! I know that some people don't like breakfast, or they are too busy and have no time to make it. That's why I've prepared four easy and delicious morning meals that will make you feel satisfied and ready for your day!

The Fancy Spread

On a Sunday, or whenever I have time for a fancy breakfast, I opt for what I call the buffet! I prepare something very similar to the wonderful spreads that hotels offer: pancakes, hash browns, beans, eggs, and roasted tomatoes. I pair all of this with a cat-puccino and orange juice—it's so delicious. Eating breakfast like this once a week will create a new tradition you can look forward to each week. Trust your good ol' friend Stanis!

The Quick Toastie

Okay, you're rushing, you really need to go, but you also need to eat! When I'm in a rush, I go for toasted bread with peanut butter and jam (I love strawberry) or a grilled cheese if I'm in the mood for something savory. Nothing beats toasted bread with add-ons! Don't forget to wash it down with some coffee or a smoothie to give you extra energy!

The Vitamin Boost

Maybe you ate too much the night before, or you just want to give yourself an extra boost of vitamins and energy. What should you eat? Fruit is the answer! I usually eat some light, plain yogurt with fresh berries (add some nuts or coconut flakes, as well, for healthy fats), or I prepare a smoothie I tried on one of my trips around the world made of blueberries, peanut butter, oat milk, and bananas.

The Extra Sweet

I'll admit, I love to go to the bakery (*very* often). I'm a lover of baked goods, and I'm probably not the only one. That's why one of my favorite breakfasts (which I know you're going to love) is based on tempting and scrumptious pastries: muffins, cupcakes, croissants with delicious fillings, and pies! They're not just for afternoons or desserts but also for mornings that need a little extra sugar! And it's very easy to pop some pastries in the freezer or pick them up over the weekend or at the beginning of the week so that they're ready to go whenever you need them.

@stanisthecat
STANIS RECIPES
SUGAR
JAM
SOAP

STANIS' RECIPES
COOKIES
SALT
SANDWICH SPREAD
Cheese

Snacking with Stanis

As a cat, I love to eat throughout the day. Having little snacks here and there helps keep me going! So if your stomach is growling, what should you do? Don't worry, because your good ol' Stanis has prepared for you lots of ideas for healthy and yummy snacks that you can cook up in just a few minutes! Salty or sweet, I've covered it all. Let's get snacking!

Bread and hazelnut butter—but I, of course, make it with very fancy add-ons and twists. For example, after I toast the bread and spread the hazelnut butter (you can opt for dark chocolate spread as well), I sprinkle coconut flakes or chopped hazelnuts on top. My final touch is a tiny pinch of salt.

Air-fried chickpeas are a great snack! Place the chickpeas on the air fryer tray, coat them in olive oil, paprika, garlic powder, and salt and black pepper, and then fry them for eight to ten minutes, or until they're at peak crispiness. These are the purrfect choice, since they're healthy and so delicious!

Salty cucumbers are so easy and quick, I make them whenever I'm in a rush (yes, it's true, cats can be in a hurry too!). I simply slice the cucumbers into little sticks, sprinkle on some salt, and off I go, eating something delicious, savory, and most of all, refreshing!

A Stanis Sandwich is made with two slices of soft bread and a lovely filling! Toasted or not, rich or simple, a sandwich saves the day. I make mine with a zingy sandwich spread, a slice of cheese, some arugula, and a thinly sliced tomato. I love it with avocado or cucumber as well!

STANIS'S TIP: If you're only a little peckish, try some nuts and dried fruit: almonds, hazelnuts, walnuts, dates, raisins, or cashews. They're a great source of vitamins, minerals, and fiber and are purrfect for a quick snack!

SALT
OLIO
@stanisthecat
OREGANO
STANIS' RECIPES

Stanis's Yummy Sides

I love veggies so much. Whenever I go to the market, I always make sure to buy enough for a smart meal prep and to enjoy the best seasonal produce! I have four staples that my friends know me for, and so I absolutely need to share them with you! They're purrfect for a nice veggie spread or to pair with your main dishes! Let's get cooking!

Wine Cabbage

Ingredients

2 tablespoons (30 milliliters) olive oil
2 garlic cloves
1 dried red chili pepper
½ head green cabbage (cut into thin strips, core discarded)
½ cup (120 milliliters) dry white wine
Salt and black pepper

How to Prepare

1. Pour the olive oil into a large pan over medium heat. Add the garlic cloves and chili pepper.
2. When the garlic and chili pepper are fragrant, add the cabbage and stir for 5 minutes, ensuring the ingredients don't burn.
3. Pour in the white wine, add the salt to taste, and stir vigorously.
4. Cover with a lid and cook on medium low for about 20 minutes.
5. Finish with the black pepper to taste and serve warm. Enjoy!

Stanis's Caponata

Ingredients

3 tablespoons (30 milliliters) olive oil, plus extra for finishing
1 red onion, chopped
2 tablespoons capers
3 eggplants, diced
2 zucchinis, diced
3 red bell peppers, diced
¼ cup (60 milliliters) dry white wine
Salt
2 tablespoons (34 grams) tomato paste
1 teaspoon oregano

How to Prepare

1. Pour the 3 tablespoons of olive oil into a large pan over medium heat. Add the onion and capers and cook for 3 to 4 minutes.
2. Add the eggplants, zucchinis, and peppers and stir well.
3. Cook the vegetables for about 5 minutes, pour in the wine, and stir again. Add the salt to taste.
4. Reduce the temperature to low and cook for 20 to 25 minutes (or longer for deeper flavor).
5. Add in the tomato paste and oregano and mix well.
6. Finish with the remaining olive oil before serving.

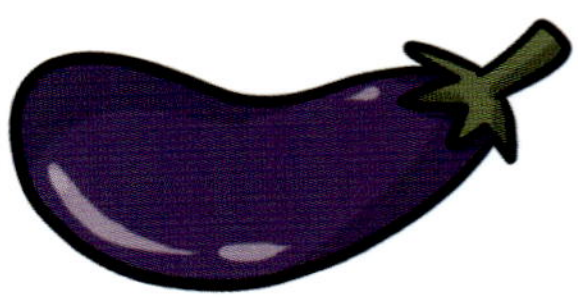

Zingy Zucchini

Ingredients

4 large zucchinis, cut into thick slices
3 tablespoons (30 milliliters) olive oil, plus extra for finishing
Salt
2 tablespoons (30 milliliters) white wine vinegar
2 garlic cloves, crushed
Fresh mint leaves, chopped

How to Prepare

1. Preheat the oven to 400°F (200°C).
2. Arrange the zucchini slices on a baking sheet without overlapping.
3. Drizzle the zucchini slices with the 3 tablespoons of olive oil and sprinkle with the salt to taste.
4. Roast the slices for 20 to 25 minutes in the oven, until they are lightly browned.
5. Set aside the zucchini to cool off, then transfer to a large bowl.
6. Add the vinegar, garlic, and mint, and finish with the remaining olive oil.
7. Stir and let sit for 2 hours for flavors to develop.
8. Serve!

Stanis's Potato Salad

Ingredients

2¾ cups (500 grams) fingerling potatoes
2 tablespoons (30 milliliters) olive oil
Salt and black pepper
½ pound (225 grams) green beans, whole or chopped
1 red onion, thinly sliced
1 tablespoon (15 milliliters) white wine vinegar
¼ cup combined fresh chopped chives, parsley, and basil
½ cup (90 grams) sliced black olives

For the dressing

1 teaspoon mustard
2 tablespoons (30 milliliters) olive oil
½ teaspoon dried dill
Salt and black pepper

How to Prepare

1. Roast the potatoes with the olive oil and a pinch of the salt at 350°F (180°C) for 30 minutes.
2. Boil the green beans for 15 minutes, then set aside.
3. Toss the onion slices with the vinegar to soften their flavor.
4. Let the potatoes cool, then transfer to a large bowl.
5. Add the herbs, onion, green beans, and olives.
6. To make the dressing, whisk together the mustard, olive oil, dill, and salt and black pepper to taste.
7. Pour the dressing over the salad, toss well, and serve!

STANIS'S PURRFECT BARBECUE

One of my favorite outdoor activities is hosting barbecues during the spring, summer, and even early autumn! Corinna and I always try to take care of our guests in the best possible way, whipping up delicious salads and grilling the best vegetables. My friends and I don't eat meat (only fish, and my favorite is tuna), so our barbecues are always vegetarian or with grilled fish! Come join the fun!

Pasta Salads Are the Trick!

While the burgers, sausages, and skewers are on the grill, you need to nibble on something, right? I always make my pasta salad with my own paws, with fresh tomatoes, black and green olives, mozzarella cut in cubes, thinly cut arugula, oil, and basil leaves. The nice thing about a pasta salad is that you can make it with whatever you have in your fridge or cupboard. Another favorite of mine? Artichokes, sun-dried tomatoes, and mushrooms!

The Drinks? Fresh and Fruity!

Whenever I host a barbecue, I also make sure to create refreshing and yummy drinks for my guests. A nice punch with coconut water, pineapple juice, and lemon soda can make the best piña colada-inspired drink (adding mint is my final touch). I'm an Italian cat, so a spritz is a must! Make it with three parts of Prosecco, two parts of Aperol, a dash of soda water, and a slice of orange. Orange like the sunset and sweet, this drink is purrfect while I'm waiting for my vegetable skewers to be ready, chatting with my friends.

Let's Play!

My friends and I play lots of games during my barbecues, and two of our favorites are charades and Jenga. We laugh so much! If you want to sit down around the table, you can't go wrong with card games: Uno is a classic, or you can play cribbage, which I've recently discovered, a game of cards great for two people. You set a target number (often 121) and deal out a deck of cards, then take turns laying down cards. The player who reaches the target number wins! Two board games I have fun with are Yahtzee or Man, Don't Get Angry (a cross and circle game in which each player has four pieces that need to travel on the board in order to reach their safe destination), but for those, you need to have the board game already on hand. They both utilize dice, which I could play with for hours!

OLIO
SALT
@stanisthecat
KETCHUP
MAYO

@stanisthecat

Stanis's Iconic Italian Aperitivo

Or as I call it: **apurritivo**! It's that time when you just unwind, drink, and snack before dinner. Yes, it sounds odd, but the Italian aperitivo gets you ready for supper, and all the Italian cats do it. At a cute little bar or from the comfort of your home, the aperitivo is a moment of relaxation to enjoy with friends or alone. Let me tell you how to do in proper Stanis style!

When I do it at home, I usually prepare one of my showy charcuterie boards using a nice wood cutting board (the bigger the better), and place **green olives**, **mini pizzas** with the yummiest tomato sauce, **cheese** cut in triangles, and **fruit** on the tray. Then, I love to pair either grapes or strawberries for a fresh bite in between. But you can add anything you want: **almonds**, **focaccia** cut in little squares, **olive tapenade**, **hummus**, or **cream cheese** to spread on rustic bread. The options are infinite!

For drinks, you have plenty of choices: **wine**, **beer**, **cocktails**, or **nonalcoholic spirits**. The star of the show is the iconic Aperol spritz, or better yet, **Apurrol spritz**! It's the drink of choice for millions of cats where I live, and I'm pretty sure the choice of many of you as well!

What to do during the apurritivo? Relax, of course, living *la dolce vita!* I know a thing or two about that, and when I'm with my friends, enjoying the sunset with a little drink in my paw, everything just feels so good! Try it on your own, with your pets, or with your family. This time before dinner is so precious and an occasion to have kind of a double dinner! Who could resist?!

STANIS'S TIP: You can also go for an easier way of doing the aperitivo, which is without the charcuterie board but instead with bowls of chips, olives, and some peanuts! Quicker but still super fun!

OLIO
VINO

STANIS'S SOUP FOR WHEN YOU FEEL UNDER THE WEATHER

Making soup is one of the sweetest and most endearing kitchen activities! It also happens to be one of my favorite things to make in the kitchen (along with pizza and tomato sauce)! Over the years, I've purrfected my very own "Stanis's soup," the one I love to savor when I'm feeling a little sick (hello, winter colds) or just when I need a tasty hug; plus, it's fully vegan and super healthy! So put on your apron and let's soup! Makes two to three bowls.

Ingredients

3 tablespoons (45 milliliters) extra virgin olive oil
1 red onion, cubed
2 garlic cloves, minced
1 leek, sliced
3 big potatoes, cut into chunks
4 carrots, sliced
1 cup (200 milliliters) water
Fresh parsley
Salt and black pepper

How to Prepare

1. Pour the olive oil into a deep pot over medium heat, add the onion and garlic, and let them sizzle for a couple of minutes.
2. Add the leek, potatoes, and carrots and stir for no more than a minute.
3. Add the water, fully covering the vegetables. Let the soup simmer for 2 hours, checking on it regularly and adding more water if needed. The vegetables should develop a creamy texture.
4. Once the vegetables are fully cooked, add the fresh parsley, a pinch or two of salt, and the black pepper, to taste.

STANIS'S TIP: Toast some bread in the oven to accompany this delicious soup. Take a few slices and rub some garlic on them, then place in the oven until golden and toasted. Pour some fresh olive oil over it (and sprinkle some nice, flaky salt or freshly cracked black pepper, if you have some) when it's still warm. A true delight!

SALE
ORIGANO
OLIO
STANIS' PLAYLIST
@stanisthecat

THE PURRFECT TOMATO SAUCE

This is my recipe for the thickest, most delicious, and yummy tomato sauce. In Italian, we call it *sugo*, and I just love to smell it on the streets when I stroll around my city.

Ingredients

Olive oil
1 large red onion, thinly sliced
3 garlic cloves, thinly sliced
2 pounds (or 3 cans) fresh San Marzano tomatoes
Salt
1 teaspoon oregano
1 bunch chopped fresh parsley
4 to 5 fresh basil leaves

How to Prepare

1. Pour the olive oil into a large, deep pan, enough to cover the base (don't be shy!) over medium heat. Make sure the oil gets warm, as it's good to get a little sizzle.
2. Place the onion and garlic into the pan, then cook until fragrant.
3. Add the tomatoes, then add the salt to taste.
4. Stir vigorously, then add the oregano, the fresh parsley, and the fresh basil.
5. Cover and let cook on low for about an hour. Stir regularly to avoid the sauce sticking to the pan.
6. The longer you cook it, the better it will be! Once you've reached the desired consistency (very creamy), enjoy it with fusilli or spaghetti!

STANIS'S TIP: Use only garlic and no onion, then add hot pepper flakes or fresh chili and lots of parsley if you want to make it *arrabbiata*.

PASTA
LOVER
DESSERTS
COOKIES
OLIO
@stanisthecat

FRESH TAGLIATELLE MADE WITH MY OWN PAWS

Oh, my dear pasta, how much I love you! Dried or fresh, pasta is undoubtedly the comfort food par excellence (alongside pizza, to be honest). A steaming, rich plate of pasta makes me feel all warm and fuzzy inside, and I'm 100% sure that I'm not the only cat who feels this way. When Sunday morning arrives, or when I have a little extra time, I like to make my very own Stanis's pasta—pawmade with love! My shape of choice? Tagliatelle, but I have so many more to introduce you to. *Andiamo!*

Ingredients (with eggs)

3¼ cups (400 grams) 00 flour
4 fresh eggs
Salt

How to Prepare

1. Create a little volcano with the flour on your work area.
2. Beat the eggs in a plate and add the egg mixture into the flour volcano's center, adding a pinch of salt.
3. Work the dough slowly to let the egg be absorbed by the flour.
4. Knead the dough like me and millions of other cats do (aka, make biscuits!).
5. When the dough looks firm, uniform, and purrfect, wrap it in plastic wrap and let it rest in the fridge for at least 30 minutes.

(Continued on next page.)

Ingredients (without eggs)

4 cups (500 grams) durum wheat flour or semolina

Pinch of salt

1 cup (250 grams) water

2 tablespoons (30 milliliters) olive oil

How to Prepare

1. Put the flour, salt, and water in a big bowl, combining them slowly and steadily, adding the water in two steps until the dough is soft and consistent.
2. Add the olive oil slowly, until the dough is firm.
3. Wrap the dough in plastic wrap for 30 minutes and let it sit without putting it in the fridge.

Let's Make the Pasta Shapes!

Tagliatelle, pappardelle, lasagna, or thin spaghetti—you can make so many shapes with the pasta dough you just made! Make sure to lay the pasta dough thin, though you can make it slightly thicker for more texture (not too thick, otherwise the pasta will take too long to cook and will stay tough).

For Easy Tagliatelle

1. Lay the pasta dough as thin as possible.
2. Loosely roll the sheet of pasta.
3. With a knife, cut the rolled sheet into centimeter-wide strips.
4. Unroll the strips and, voilà, here's your tagliatelle!

Time to Eat!

Now boil some water with salt and throw your pasta in (only when the water has bubbles bubbling!) and let it cook for a few minutes; my best tip is to always try to make sure you're reaching the right consistency, which should be al dente! Pair your tagliatelle with my tomato sauce for the best pasta dish ever, or you can make your own sauce with porcini mushrooms and cream, or with pesto!

FOUR WHISKER-WORTHY PASTA DISHES

As an Italian cat, pasta is always on my menu! I eat it practically every day, and it gives me all the energy and flavor I need. Let me unveil my top four recipes (which I always make for my friends) so you can try them even as a newcomer to cooking your own pasta!

Fusilli with Zucchini, Mint, and Lemon Zest

This is such a light and refreshing pasta dish. It tastes like summer!

Ingredients

4 tablespoons (60 milliliters) olive oil
2 large zucchinis, sliced
1 large red onion, chopped
Salt
Handful fresh mint leaves
1 pound (450 grams) fusilli pasta, cooked, with water reserved
Lemon zest
Parmesan (optional)

How to Prepare

1. Pour the olive oil into a medium pan over medium heat.
2. Add the zucchini and onion and let cook for about 10 minutes, until soft and browned. Add the salt to taste.
3. Add the mint leaves and stir.
4. Toss in the cooked pasta, the lemon zest to taste, and 2 tablespoons (30 milliliters) of the pasta water, stirring until creamy.
5. Add some Parmesan for extra zing!

PASTA
PACCHERI
PASTA
@stanisthecat

Pappardelle with Porcini Mushrooms

A Sunday favorite of mine, especially during the cold months!

Ingredients

$1\frac{2}{3}$ cups (250 grams) dried or fresh porcini mushrooms
4 tablespoons (60 milliliters) olive oil
3 cloves garlic
Handful fresh parsley
Drizzle of dry white wine
Salt
1 pound (450 grams) cooked pappardelle
Parmesan, grated

How to Prepare

1. Soak the dried porcini mushrooms in hot water for about 1 hour (skip if using fresh).
2. Pour the olive oil into a large pan over medium heat, adding the garlic, the mushrooms, and the parsley.
3. Pour in the white wine and continue to cook over medium heat to let the wine evaporate, then lower the temperature and cook for 10 to 15 minutes, until tender. Add the salt to taste.
4. Add the pappardelle and stir over low heat. Finish with lots of Parmesan!

Spaghetti with Sun-Dried Tomatoes and Almonds

Quick, easy, and incredibly delicious! I make this anytime I have guests over (Corinna *loves* this) and I want to surprise them with something yummy and easy for me to make.

Ingredients

- 4 tablespoons (60 milliliters) olive oil
- 2 to 3 garlic cloves
- A few handfuls of almonds (flakes or chunks)
- 4 ounces sun-dried tomatoes
- Salt
- 1 pound (450 grams) cooked spaghetti
- Handful fresh parsley

How to Prepare

1. Pour the olive oil into a medium-size pan over medium heat, then add the garlic and almonds and sauté for 2 minutes.
2. Add the sun-dried tomatoes, reduce the temperature to low, and cook for 5 minutes. Add the salt to taste.
3. Toss in the spaghetti, stir well, and finish with the parsley. Stanis approved!

Paccheri with Roasted Eggplant

This shape of pasta is big like my paw and I love it! I usually make a hearty eggplant sauce to go with it, and it's simply delicious

Ingredients

2 large eggplants, cubed
3 tablespoons (45 milliliters) olive oil, plus some for drizzling
Salt
2 cloves garlic
17 ounces (500 grams) tomato sauce (fresh or passata)
1 teaspoon oregano
Handful fresh basil, roughly chopped
1 pound (450 grams) paccheri
Grating of salted ricotta

How to Prepare

1. Preheat the oven to 400°F.
2. Place the eggplant on a tray and cover with the 3 tablespoons of olive oil, and add the salt to taste, then roast in the oven for 20 minutes.
3. In a large pan over medium heat, add the remaining olive oil, and then add the garlic and roasted eggplant and stir for about 5 minutes.
4. Add in the tomato sauce, oregano, and basil. Cook on low heat for 30 minutes.
5. Toss with the paccheri and finish with the salted ricotta—enjoy!

Stanis's Festive Bites

Hosting is a favorite pastime of mine! When the holidays approach (Christmas, Easter, New Year's Eve, etc.), I can't help but start making up menus and saving ideas here and there on my MeowPhone. I have plenty of recipe books for help too! So holiday after holiday, I have created and purrfected my very own little Stanis's appetizers menu to enjoy together with friends and family at a large, happy table!

Puff Pastry Christmas Tree

This is an easy and good-looking appetizer for all ages! You can make a sweet version of this, too, by substituting chocolate-hazelnut spread for the pesto, and coconut flakes for the cherry tomatoes!

Ingredients

2 puff pastry sheets
¾ cup (200 grams) pesto
1 cup (200 grams) sliced cherry tomatoes

How to Prepare

1. Lay a sheet of puff pastry on a tray and cut out a large triangle for the tree, including a vertical rectangle at the base.
2. Cut out a little star shape and set aside for later.
3. Spread a thin layer of the pesto on the tree and place the second puff pastry sheet on top, trimming it to match the underlying tree shape.
4. Cut half-inch to inch-long (2- to 3-centimeter) branches on both sides of the tree, leaving the middle intact.
5. Twist and twirl branches together, and add cherry tomatoes as ornaments.
6. Finally, place the star on top.

Bruschetta Spread

Who doesn't love bread with delicious stuff on top? Here is a selection of my staples!

TOMATOES

Marinate cube-cut tomatoes with olive oil, minced garlic, roughly chopped red onions, basil, and salt. Let it sit for a couple of hours in the fridge and then serve on toasted bread.

MUSHROOMS

Cook mushrooms cut in half in white wine, butter (or margarine), garlic, and parsley. Let the wine reduce a bit to create a little creamy texture. Then place on warm bread with shaved Parmesan.

HUMMUS AND GRILLED VEGETABLES

Make homemade hummus by blending a pot of chickpeas, a teaspoon of paprika, one teaspoon of garlic powder, a drizzle of oil, your favorite herbs (mine are parsley and dill, either fresh or dried), and half a teaspoon of lemon juice. Add cumin, as well, if you like a richer taste. Blend everything and add a little hot water at the very end for a creamier texture. Grill zucchini, bell pepper, and eggplant and, when done, place a generous layer of hummus on toasted bread and the grilled veggies on top!

Mushroom Panzerotti

Small and delicious, these are truly tiny pockets of happiness!

Ingredients

- 3⅓ cups (500 grams) mixed mushrooms
- 5 tablespoons (75 milliliters) olive oil
- 2 cloves garlic
- 5 teaspoons (25 grams) cream cheese
- Parmesan, grated
- Handful fresh parsley
- Handful fresh chives
- 2 sheets puff pastry
- 2 teaspoons sesame seeds

How to Prepare

1. Place the mushrooms in a medium-size pan over medium heat and sauté with 3 tablespoons of the olive oil, the garlic, cream cheese, Parmesan to taste, parsley, and chives. Reduce the temperature and let cool.
2. Cut large circles from the puff pastry, big enough to hold the mushroom ragout.
3. Place a spoonful of the mushroom ragout in the center of each circle and fold the pastry over it to create half-moon shapes, sealing the edges by pressing with a fork.
4. Brush the tops with the remaining olive oil.
5. Sprinkle with the sesame seeds.
6. Bake at 325°F (160°C) for 20 to 25 minutes. Increase to 350°F (180°C) for the last 5 minutes for a golden finish.
7. Let the panzerotti sit for a few minutes before enjoying!

Even More . . .

Together with these cute appetizers I always make for special occasions, I pair delicious tiny bites like olives (I love them so much!), crackers with cheeses and jams, veggie spreads, and salads! It's always a smart idea, as you can easily put together a complete dinner like this—no need for main courses, just the joy of nibbling and sharing with many paws having fun.

SOAP
@stanisthecat
COCOA POWDER
SUGAR
Stanis
TIRAMISÙ

Stanis's Famous Tirameowsu

When the weather is a little meh, or my day feels a little slow, I know one thing that can make it all go right: tirameowsu! In Italian, tiramisu (*tirami su*) means literally "pick me up" and, boy, it sure does! I prepare it for big occasions too. All my friends love it, so prepare your paws to make some good ol' espresso, and let's make one of the best desserts out there!

Ingredients

4 large eggs
½ cup (100 grams) sugar
14 ounces (400 grams) mascarpone cheese
10½ ounces (300 grams) savoiardi (ladyfingers)
4 cups (950 milliliters) espresso, cooled
⅓ cup (40 grams) sweetened cocoa powder

STANIS'S TIP: You can modify the tiramisu with any fruit or ingredient you like! Strawberry, pistachio, raspberries, lemon, or even coconut! Just let your imagination run wild!

How to Prepare

1. Separate the egg yolks from the egg whites (setting aside the whites to use later) and beat the egg yolks with the sugar until the consistency becomes creamy and soft.
2. Stir in the mascarpone cheese until nice and smooth.
3. In another bowl, beat the egg whites until foamy and cloudy and add them to the egg-and-cheese mixture, mixing well to form a cream.
4. Dip the savoiardi into the espresso and arrange in a layer on a large rectangular tray. Top with a layer of cream. Repeat, adding a layer of savoiardi and a layer of cream.
5. Sprinkle the cocoa powder on top and let the dessert rest in the fridge for at least 3 hours.

PIZZA NIGHT
FLOUR
TOMATO

IT'S PIZZA NIGHT!

Are you hungry? Time for pizza! Are you feeling sad and in need of a scrumptious bite? Time for pizza! You need to celebrate something special? Time for (you guessed it) pizza! Pizza is truly the answer to every question. I love to make my own dough and host a delicious pizza night at my house together with my friends. As you probably know, I have to knead a lot for a fine and soft pizza dough, but that's my specialty! My paws are very experienced! But the best part is what goes on top! Let me share with you my favorite toppings for a Stanis-approved pizza night!

The Veggies

I love to eat vegetables as much as I can, so don't get me started on how much I love them on pizza! I combine radicchio, potatoes, and Parmesan shavings with a drizzle of olive oil on a white base with mozzarella. This is cozy and purrfect for autumn nights. During summer, I like to pair zucchini and cherry tomatoes, also on a white base of mozzarella (here, I add a little black pepper for a tiny zing), and finally my favorite red sauce-based pizza with onicn, black olives, and a mountain of arugula!

The Quirkiest

It's fun to get creative with pizza toppings, but as an Italian cat, I'll always be a little doubtful about pineapple. Still, there are some quirky pizzas I've tried and thought, *Hey, That was amazing!* even if they were a little out of my comfort zone. For example, I was skeptical of pizza with peaches, burrata, and rosemary—but when I tried it, it was so yummy! In Rome, during September, we always eat pizza bianca (flatbread with salt and oil) with fresh-picked figs. It's so delicious!

The Gourmets

Classy pizza, anyone? Yes, please! Porcini mushrooms and oven-roasted potatoes on a white base of mozzarella is one of my top choices when I'm feeling a little fancy. If you like strong flavors, though, add some shaved truffles (or truffle oil) on top. I love dried tomatoes so much, so I put them on top of my pizza as well! Together with some shaved Parmesan cheese (or Pecorino cheese for a bolder taste), pesto, and melted mozzarella, it is just so good!

STANIS'S TIP: In Rome, we have shops that sell pizza by the slice (called *al taglio*), which is great inspiration for an amazing pizza night at home! You can make plenty of differently flavored pizzas in the shape of rectangles (big or small, depending on how hungry you are and how many friends and family you have invited) and enjoy a little Roman feast in your own house!

ACKNOWLEDGMENTS

This book is proof of what happens when you don't lose hope, when kindness shows up and doesn't give up on you. In this book, there are so many hearts and paws other than just mine and Stanis's. Every page of this book, every illustration, every small detail holds an enormous amount of love, hard work, and excitement. *Stanis's Guide to a Purrfect Life* exists because so many people believed in it, and Stanis and I couldn't be more grateful. Thanks to the one and only Stanis, my cat, for the immense inspiration; my husband, Rik, for his unwavering support, even on the hardest days; my whole family; my agent, Jon (special thanks to his cat Charles, who was very present through the whole process as well!), my editor Katie, and the whole team at Andrews McMeel (I couldn't have asked for a better publishing house to be working with on this special project). Stanis would love to write a couple of words too: "Thank you, my furriends, for giving me the chance to make your days brighter, one gentle, cozy adventure after the other. Thanks to you with this book in your paws and to everyone who helped turn this dream into reality."

Lots of love from a round black cat, with very big purrs of thanks for everyone who made this book possible.

With love,
Elisa & Stanis

ABOUT THE AUTHORS

Elisa Colarossi is a Rome-based illustrator whose artistic career was reignited during the 2020 lockdown, thanks to the whimsical and heartwarming adventures of her black cat, Stanis. Born in 1991 and raised in the Eternal City, Elisa gained widespread attention after her illustrations of Stanis went viral, being featured on platforms like Bored Panda, *Esquire*, *Wanted in Rome*, *Romeing*, and *Italia!* magazine. As an illustrator and storyteller, she uses her art not only to entertain but to remind people of the joy that can be found in the simplest things—a message that resonates deeply in our times.

As for the *real* author, Stanis was born in the bustling streets of Rome and found his human in 2013. He has proved since then that he is no ordinary cat, thanks to his knowledge on cozy naps, expertise on windowsill lounging, and more, which he decided to share through the whimsical illustrations of his human. When he is not kneading pasta, Stanis is busy exploring new hobbies and activities, and he loves to spend time with his friends, proving that even the most snuggly cats can lead vibrant lives!